C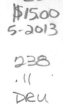MMON GROUND

COMMON GROUND

What All Christians Believe and Why It Matters

KEITH DRURY

wesleyan
publishing
house

Indianapolis, Indiana

Copyright © 2008 by Keith Drury
Published by Wesleyan Publishing House
Indianapolis, Indiana 46250
Printed in the United States of America
ISBN: 978-0-89827-354-0

Library of Congress Cataloging-in-Publication Data

Drury, Keith W.
 Common ground : what all Christians believe and why it matters / Keith
Drury.
    p. cm.
 Includes bibliographical references and index.
 ISBN 978-0-89827-354-0 (alk. paper)
 1. Christianity--Essence, genius, nature. 2. Theology, Doctrinal. I.
Title.
 BT60.D755 2008
 238'.11--dc22
                                        2008007588

To Paul Kind and Mark Schmerse,
Companions on the trail and in the church

CONTENTS

ACKNOWLEDGMENTS

Writing a book on the Apostles' Creed is harder than it sounds. I am neither a theologian nor a Bible scholar. I am a minister, and teach practical ministry to ministerial students. Yet over the years, I have come to see the importance of the core Christian doctrines upon which we all agree—the unchanging things.

Several years ago, I began researching for this book, and today I am turning in the nineteenth draft. It still is not a perfect book, but it would not be even what it is now without the help of dedicated and generous scholars who have read and reviewed the manuscript—some of them several times over. I offer grateful thanks to theologian Chris Bounds for reading the manuscript in its earliest stages and offering corrections and suggestions—especially on important strains of thought I had omitted. Bible scholars Ken Schenck, David Smith, and Steve Lennox offered helpful insights from a biblical perspective that I would never have seen on my own and that did not emerge even from my extensive research. Scientist Burt Webb helped me with technical foundations of chapter 2. Tamara Bounds read the manuscript as a layperson and offered a host of suggestions to make the book more readable and understandable. Larry Wilson, my editor, suggested numerous structural changes that improved the work considerably, along with offering superb editing of the final draft.

My family was also involved. Young theologian John Drury offered numerous helpful suggestions; as did my other son, David Drury, who read the book from a pastor's point of view; and my wife, Sharon, generously did a complete edit of the manuscript near the end of my writing process.

Along with assistance gained from these people, I received help from a number of good books. There are dozens of great books on the Apostles' Creed, and I studied many of them in my year of research before writing. Most Christian thinkers (and almost all theologians) have written on the creeds. Augustine's *Sermon to Catechumens* and his *Treatise on Faith and the Creed* were seminal—both for the church and for me. Thomas Aquinas gave a series on the creed shortly before his death, and they were extremely insightful ("The Sermon-conferences of St. Thomas on the Apostles' Creed"). In Martin Luther's *Large Catechism* I found the most concentrated teaching on the creed. He packed more great ideas in fewer words than anyone I read. Karl Barth's early work, *Dogmatics in Outline*, offered deep insights as always. I also studied more recent writers' works on the creeds, notably Luke Timothy Johnson's *The Creed*, which helped me see the creeds in light of today's world. Hans Urs von Balthasar's

Credo: Meditations on the Apostles' Creed inspired me to reflect on love as God's motivation for His work and in theology. These were primary influences on my writing.

Besides these primary works, I should acknowledge several other books, including Alister McGrath's *I Believe: Exploring the Apostles' Creed*, Wolfhart Pannenberg's *The Apostles' Creed in Light of Today's Questions*, William Barclay's bulky writing in *The Apostles' Creed*, Emil Brunner's sermons on the creed published as *I Believe in the Living God*, Roger Van Harn's *Exploring and Proclaiming the Apostles' Creed*, and a recent work for younger readers by Ray Pritchard titled *Credo: Believing in Something to Die For*. These books combined to keep me within the circle of common ground where Christians agree. Thank you to both my scholarly colleagues who read the manuscript and to these brilliant Christian writers who inspired me as I read and wrote. Writing this book led me to greater devotion and worship. I hope reading it will do the same for you.

KEITH DRURY
March 8, 2008

11

WHY WE STUDY
THE APOSTLES' CREED

This book is for Christians who seldom recite the creed in worship, never learned the creed, or cannot repeat it without reading the words from a book or worship folder. This book is written with the conviction that our beliefs are important and ought to be studied—especially those beliefs that form the common ground we hold with all Christians past and present. So if you come from a non-creedal tradition, here are several reasons why it is important for you to understand the creeds in general and the Apostles' Creed in particular.

THE CREED UNDERLINES THE BIBLE

Creeds do not replace the Bible but underscore its essential doctrines. They highlight the most important doctrines in the Bible—upon which we all agree.

Not all Bible verses are of equal weight. For example, there are more verses about speaking in tongues than on the virgin birth, but that does not mean speaking in tongues is more important than the virgin birth. We do not get our doctrine using arithmetic to add up the verses on a particular subject and calculate what matters most. The Holy Spirit guided early Christians to recognize certain core doctrines and put them into a creed. The Apostles' Creed reminds us of the most vital doctrines in the Bible. It is doctrinal concentrate.

In later creeds, the church became more talkative. This book focuses primarily on the Apostles' Creed, though it sometimes refers to the more intricate Nicene Creed to expand and explain the shorter Apostles' Creed. The creeds are a sort of theological *Reader's Digest* that underscores the most important doctrines of the Bible.

Knowing the core claims of Christianity should be important to Christians.

THE CREED STATES MINIMUM BELIEFS

The creeds are sparse and thus provide a statement of the minimum beliefs for a Christian. The creeds leave out many doctrines that are the specialties of various denominations. That is the genius of the creeds: they provide us with the bare minimum of Christian belief. You can be a Christian and not accept the doctrines of eternal security or speaking in tongues or entire sanctification, but you cannot be a Christian and reject the core doctrines in the creeds. Every Christian ought to believe more than what is stated in the Apostles' Creed; however, no Christian should believe less. We should study the creed to remind ourselves of the core beliefs upon which all Christians agree—the minimum belief required to call oneself Christian.

THE CREED DEFINES HERESY

The creeds both provide the inner core of doctrine and define the outer limits of beliefs. They delineate what is doctrinally out-of-bounds. If a person says, "I think Jesus never really came back from the dead—he just was in a coma," the Apostles' Creed sets off an alarm bell among Christians. We disagree about lots of things in the Bible, and we are generous to those with whom we differ. However, we fully agree about the statements in the creed. When someone rejects a creedal doctrine, we are not supposed to be casual about it. Doctrine matters, especially core doctrine. The creed is our referee on the playing field of theology. With so many secular books and television shows focusing on religious issues, we need to know the doctrinal boundaries so we can identify heresy and hold tightly to the sound doctrines of the Bible.

15

THE CREED UNITES US

Creeds emphasize our common ground with other Christians. Baptists, Wesleyans, and Roman Catholics disagree on many things, but we unanimously agree on the creeds. Denominations tend to emphasize their differences with one another, which presents a divided front to the world. The world says, "You can't even agree among yourselves; how can you talk to us about truth?" However, we do agree on the vital doctrines in the creeds. So studying the Apostles' Creed helps us emphasize our common beliefs to the world—and to ourselves. Studying the creeds is unifying.

THE CREED HAS A LONG HISTORY

The creeds are our anchor to the historic Christian faith. The Apostles' Creed probably began as a list of questions asked of baptismal candidates. However, such an affirmation of faith needed to be more than a once-for-all-time statement reserved for new believers. So Christians began repeating the creed every week as part of worship. Most have done so ever since, with some modern-day exceptions. The Nicene Creed came later and is the earliest official creed established at a universal council of the church. It expands and adds detail to the core statements in the simpler Apostles' Creed.

16
The Apostles' Creed is more popular and easier to memorize; it is the shortest full-length creed. Its origin has been attributed to the apostles, but that is unlikely. The Apostles' Creed did originate very early in the church's history and essentially represents what the apostles taught and wrote in the Bible. When we study (and recite) the creeds, we remember what Christians have always believed and

avoid cutting ourselves off from two thousand years of orthodox Christianity. Studying the creeds reminds us of the things on which Christians everywhere at all times and in all places agree. The creeds are the roots of our theological family tree.

THE CREED SHOWS US WHAT IS
WORTH DYING FOR

The Apostles' Creed reminds us what we are willing to die for. Few of us would allow ourselves to be burned at the stake for the doctrine of eternal security or the right to ordain women. However, we would die before rejecting Jesus Christ as God. The church writes some things in pencil—they are easily erased by the next generations. Other things are written in ink—they are hard to erase because we believe them so strongly. The creeds, however, are written in *blood*. The martyrs died for these beliefs. We would too. The creeds do not change with the winds and whims of the times. If thousands of martyrs have died for these beliefs, we should at least be willing to take some time to study them.

17

THE CREED IS LIFE CHANGING

The creeds are not merely statements of boring doctrine; they affect how we live. Studying the creeds will change the way you live. Revivalist evangelicals rightfully want to avoid becoming a "dusty, musty, creedal church." We want a changed life, a vibrant daily walk with God. Yet what we believe affects how we behave.

This book specializes in showing the practical effects of our core beliefs on our daily lives. The closing section of each chapter asks, "So what about us?" If we really believe in everlasting life, it will change how we live this afternoon. Doctrine changes our outlook, our values, our worship, and the way we treat others. The creeds show us God's great plan of redemption. And the better we know God's plan of redemption, the better our worship and living will become. The popular saying "It's the deeds, not the creeds" merely points out that a statement of faith without accompanying action is dead formalism. However, the opposite is also true: deeds without creeds produce empty legalism. If living a good life were all that mattered, Buddhists, cult members, and even some atheists might rate higher than many Christians. But right living alone is not enough. Believing the right things is also important. Christlike living by people who reject Christ will not count in the end. Spirituality without theological content is an empty shell. The Christian religion emphasizes both right beliefs and right behavior. Our deeds show the world how to live, but our creeds show them whom we live for and why. Studying the creeds makes a difference in how we live.

18

WE RECITE THE CREED TOO SELDOM

The less we say the creeds in worship, the more we ought to study them. Evangelicals have stripped from their worship anything that seems "too Catholic" or "too formal." Yet we of all people believe that doctrine matters. We do not say, "Believe whatever you want to so long as you are sincere." We believe that the content of a person's faith is important. We believe doctrine matters. If we seldom recall our core beliefs by reciting the Apostles' Creed together in worship, we can at least study it in Sunday school or in small groups so that we will know what beliefs we should hold dear. This book is intended for exactly that use—to study and ponder the core doctrines that form the common ground for all Christians and always have. It is an exciting study, and it will change the way you worship and live.

19

THE APOSTLES' CREED

I believe in God the Father Almighty,

maker of heaven and earth;

And in Jesus Christ, his only Son, our Lord:

who was conceived by the Holy Spirit,

born of the Virgin Mary,

suffered under Pontius Pilate,

was crucified, dead, and buried;

he descended into hell.

The third day he rose again from the dead;

he ascended into heaven,

and sits at the right hand of God the Father Almighty;

from there he shall come to judge the living and the dead.

I believe in the Holy Spirit, the holy catholic Church, the

communion of saints, the forgiveness of sins, the resurrection

of the body, and the life everlasting.

Amen.

THE NICENE CREED

We believe in one God the Father Almighty,

maker of heaven and earth,

and of all things visible and invisible.

And in one Lord Jesus Christ,

the only-begotten Son of God,

begotten of his Father before all worlds;

God of God, Light of Light,

very God of very God,

begotten, not made,

being of one substance with the Father,

by whom all things were made;

who for us and for our salvation, came down from heaven,

and was incarnate by the Holy Spirit of the Virgin Mary,

and was made man,

and was crucified also for us under Pontius Pilate;

he suffered and was buried,

and the third day he rose again according to the Scriptures,

and ascended into heaven,

and sits at the right hand of the Father;

and he shall come again with glory to judge both the living
and the dead;
whose kingdom shall have no end.

And we believe in the Holy Spirit,
the Lord and Giver of life,
who proceeds from the Father and the Son,
who with the Father and the Son together is worshipped and
glorified;
who spoke by the prophets.

And we believe in one holy catholic and apostolic church;
We acknowledge one baptism for the remission of sins;
and we look for the resurrection of the dead,
and the life of the world to come.
Amen.

ALMIGHTY GOD

What I don't get is this: if God
is a loving Father who only
wants what's best for us, and if
he is almighty so he can do
anything he wants, then why
do bad things like cancer
happen to people? It seems
like God must be either a
loving Father who isn't all that
powerful or else an almighty
God who isn't all that good.

—Karin*

The problem of evil arises in the very first phrase of the Apostles'
Creed. The creed claims God is both a loving Father and at the
same time, he is almighty. How can he be both? We say God is
loving, yet we also claim that he can do anything. How can we
match this belief about God with our experience of a world in
which so many bad things happen?

---

*Each chapter of this book begins with a quote adapted from a real comment by a college
student, Sunday school attendee, or popular book that falls short of orthodoxy. The purpose
is to remind us that some doctrinal statements sound quite reasonable yet are unsound biblically
and theologically. The intent is not to make fun of any sincere person (the names have been
changed in any case) but to show the importance of understanding sound doctrine as outlined
in the creed.

We shall address this problem presently, but this initial phrase of the creed is packed with beautiful doctrines, and we will first examine these before asking the hard question about how a loving, all-powerful God could permit evil.

WE BELIEVE

Christians are believers. The word *creed* springs from the first word of the creed itself, the Latin word *credo*, which means "I believe." Others may scoff at the existence of God and insist that we prove he is real, but we are never able to do so to their satisfaction. We cannot prove God, we believe in God. Certainly, there is ample evidence for God—he has left his fingerprints all over creation. However, we do not have enough evidence to prove this to skeptics beyond all doubt. If we are limited to the human scientific method, the problem of God's existence will remain unresolved. However, we Christians say God does exist—we *believe* this, which is why we call ourselves believers.

Did you collect all the scientific evidence and then make a rational decision about whether or not there is a God? Few do. Most of us came to believe in God by his grace. God revealed himself to us, and we responded and believed. Likewise, we confess our belief and hope others will believe too. Intellectual proofs for God reinforce our faith but do not cause it. Only God causes faith. The atheist says, "There is no God." We say, "I believe in

God." Both are statements of faith. We believe that above all and behind all, there is a personal, loving Father. Others ridicule us, saying, "You have never seen this God; how can you say he exists?" We reply, "Credo." I believe.

WE BELIEVE IN ONE GOD

Christians believe there is only one God. We do not mean that we believe our God is the top God or best God or God-in-chief. We believe he is the only God that exists. The Nicene Creed states it this way: "We believe in one God." We are saying there is only one true God of the universe. This God is *the* God, this God is the *only* God, and this God is *my* God. We are not saying our God is equal with all the others or even better than the rest; we are saying our God is the one and only God—Father, Son, and Holy Spirit—the Creator of heaven and earth.

However, as Augustine pointed out long ago, we are saying more than this. We are not saying merely that we believe God exists or that we believe what God has said; we are saying that we believe *in* God. We trust him. We have invested our lives with God. We have bet our lives for here and for eternity on him. The creed answers the question "Who is God?" God is Father, Son, and Holy Spirit—the Holy Trinity. This is not three Gods but one God in three persons. The three sections of the creed declare what we believe about the Trinity.

27

GOD THE FATHER

If there were a paternity suit filed on behalf of creation, God would be identified as the Father. God is the Father of all. He is seminal. He is the Source of all that is seen and unseen. The early Christians did not choose to start the creed with the statement "I believe in Almighty God." They stated, "I believe in God the Father Almighty." The order is important because the fatherhood of God precedes his might. Relationship and love confront us in the very first phrase of the creed.

A PARTICULAR FATHER

Saying God is Father implies that there are children. Yet the term *father* in the creed is not used primarily in reference to us but to God's Son. When we say, "I believe in God the Father," we mean one particular father—the Father of Jesus Christ our Lord. This is a statement about the Trinity. Fathering us comes later. So the creed is clarifying what we mean when we use the word *God.* We do not mean the Father alone. Christians believe that God is the Holy Trinity—God the Father, God the Son, and God the Holy Spirit. This is not three Gods, but one. The Trinity is so hard to get our minds around that we can easily slip into referring to the Father as God and then think of Jesus as something less. Indeed, this was one of the first heresies in the church.

We shall address that later, but at this point we are reminded that the Father spoken of in the creed is the Father of Jesus Christ our Lord. The Christian God is the Holy Trinity.

A Loving Relationship

Using the term *father* to describe God indicates from the start that we have a relationship with him. Where there is a father, there must be children. We are those children. We Christians see God as something more than a distant watchmaker-type creator who designed this complex world, then wound it up and walked away. God the Father is in relationship both with his only Son and with us, his children. While there is truth in the ideas that God is a king and we are his subjects or that God is a judge and we are the accused, we Christians see God primarily as the heavenly Father with us as his children. Some people who have had poor earthly fathers are troubled by this notion. However, God's fatherhood is not merely human fatherhood written in larger letters. God is the original Father from whom all other fathering is derived (and reflects poorly). When we approach the Father, we do so in confidence that God is a person who cares about us and loves us. Christians approach God as *Abba*. God is not an impersonal force or abstract idea but is a father. He is a living, loving person. Thus, God is not distant from us but has chosen to be close to and to care for us—we relate to him intimately. How do we know this? The Bible tells us so.

A New Conception of Sin

Once we understand God as Father, a new conception of sin dawns on us. No longer do we think of sin as exclusively law breaking, as if God were merely a king or a judge. Sin is not so much about violating the law as about breaking a relationship. Sin is more about unreturned love than about broken commandments. Sin is whatever wounds God's heart. All this becomes clear to us when we understand the idea of God as Father.

A Family

When we claim God as Father, it means we have brothers and sisters. God's family is large. When we were adopted by God, we joined this extended family. He is not my Father only; he is *our* Father. We say so in the prayer Jesus taught us. God expects us to love our brothers and sisters as we love him, for how can we love God, whom we have not seen, if we do not love our brothers and sisters whom we have seen? Christians are family folk, even if we never marry another person. We inherit brothers and sisters to love and care for. We cannot claim to love God any more than we love our brothers and sisters, for Jesus taught us that this exactly how we show our love to God—by loving his other children. The fatherhood of God implies that there must be a family.

Provider

That God is Father reminds us that he is our provider. In most religions, the so-called god demands gifts from worshippers. Yet Christians know that God is the primary gift giver. Sure, we bring offerings to church, and there were offerings and sacrifices stipulated by regulations in the Old Testament; but these are not the core acts of giving in the Christian religion. It is God who performs the core giving acts in our religion. God is the number one giver. He is Jehovah Jireh—the Father-Provider. He cares for us.

All that we have can be traced upstream to our Father. He is the Source. This is called *providence*. God gives us life, a spouse, a house, a car, and our next breath. He gave us the sun and moon and the stars and seasons and mountains. Everything we have is a gift from God. He is the provider and sustainer of life. However, even these are not his greatest gifts. God loved the world so much that he gave his only begotten Son. Jesus Christ is God's greatest gift because he provided for our salvation. This is the God we Christians bet our lives on—the Father and giver of life. While it is true that we do not get every good thing we ask for, every good thing we do have comes from him.

31

Almighty

God the Father is almighty. He can do anything—he is omnipotent. In these later centuries of the Christian faith, Christians can be quite talkative about God's various characteristics, but in the early days they simply said he was almighty. God has all ability. He can do whatever he wants unless self-limited by his own will or character. The term *almighty* includes God's eternality, his infinity, and all the omni- words we use to describe him, like omnipresent, omniscient, and omnipotent. When the angel Gabriel visited Mary to announce that she would bear a child, even though she was a virgin, she asked, "How can this be?" We all need to hear Gabriel's response. He said, "Nothing is impossible with God." As the old song goes, God can do anything but fail.

This almighty God is the ruler of all creation. He existed before creation—before time itself. Our almighty God is above all laws of nature, and he cannot be arrested for any act. He stands before no court and answers to no one. He has all power, all knowledge, all might. He can do what he wishes. He could cast all of us into hell and nobody could complain. Yet this almighty, fearsome God has chosen to be our loving Father! God could have chosen not to love us, but he didn't. He chose to love. And he acted on that choice by sending his Son, Jesus Christ, to die and rise again for us and our salvation.

32

LOVING FATHER VERSUS ALMIGHTY KING

So which is it—is God more of a loving Father or an almighty king? The question that introduced this chapter is a serious puzzle. If God is indeed a loving Father, why do so many bad things happen?

If this loving God is all powerful, why would he let people die of cancer? If God could have stopped terrorists from blowing up the building where your husband worked, why didn't he? It seems like we end up with either a loving Father who is weak and cannot stop evil or an almighty God who is unloving. Either portrait of God is repellant: an ineffectual father or a cruel tyrant. Theologians call this the "problem of evil."

Solutions to the Problem of Evil

There are answers to this dilemma, of course. An answer to the problem of evil is called a *theodicy*. Many books have been written on the subject, but we will mention only a few of the answers that have been offered throughout history.

We might say that God set into motion certain laws of nature and now lets nature run its course. When a child falls from a tree, the laws of gravity play out and God does not interfere. When automobiles crash into one another, our human bodies are subject to these laws of nature and God does not interrupt. Or we might say that God has limited his will by allowing humans to make certain choices. Using that free will, they sometimes choose to strap bombs to themselves and blow up children in the marketplace, and God does not overrule their free will even when it is used to do harm. Or we might say that sin reigns on earth, at least for the time being; and wars, disease, and death are the result of the sin God has not yet destroyed. We might even say that our time on

33

earth is but a moment compared to eternity, so any pain we experience here is irrelevant compared to the glory of the next life—like pain in childbirth. We could go so far as to say that suffering is not bad at all but is actually good in the upside-down kingdom of God.

These are some of the answers people have thought of for the problem of evil, but they all seem to leave us with more questions.

Inscrutable

Perhaps the problem of evil is not solvable because God's ways are unknowable. Maybe we would not understand the answer to our question even if God did try to explain it to us. The ways of God are sometimes a mystery—he is inscrutable. Just because God is personal does not mean he can be easily understood. Maybe we will understand all of this when we see him face to face. On the other hand, maybe we will never figure it out, even in heaven. In our creeds, we do not explain things; we confess them. We do not comprehend them fully even though we believe them. Who knows the ways of God? Here on earth we know in part because we see though a glass dimly. We do our best to explain this riddle, but we never do so fully. In the poem "The Ancient Sage," Alfred Lord Tennyson put it this way: "For nothing worth proving can be proven, nor yet disproven." Some ways of God we cannot explain. We say God is both all loving and all powerful, yet we cannot fully satisfy our own questions on the matter. Still, we believe. We believe in God the Father Almighty.

Perhaps this is why so many Christians have recited this phrase every week for two thousand years. We confess our faith without sight. We trust without proof. We believe. We know God loves, and we know he can do anything. We just can't explain why he does—or doesn't do, the things we think he should. So until we get fuller answers than these, we simply believe.

WHAT ABOUT US

What shall we say, then? If God the Father Almighty loves us and can do anything, what do we do? We pray. If we did not believe he loved us, we would not ask for any good thing from him. If we did not believe he was almighty, we would have no hope for answered prayer. Yet we do believe that he is both loving and almighty, so we ask. We come before his throne boldly—like sons and daughters approaching our loving heavenly Father. We make our requests known to him and leave it at that. The fact that God does not act in any given situation does not mean that he could not act. He can do anything. We trust his judgment because we believe *in* God. We do not get all the good things we ask for; but we get some good things and we thank God for those. We believe in God regardless of what we receive.

We know, of course, that temporal requests are not all that important anyway. Mostly, we thank God for his greater gifts—salvation and eternal life. Our story does not end here on earth. We look for-

35

ward to another world that is different and better than this one. Jesus promised this, and we believe him. Even more than this, we are grateful that God so loved the world that he gave his only Son. Because we have believed in him, we shall not perish but have everlasting life. Even if we never had one other answer to prayer, we have already received the most important one. We confessed our sins, and God was faithful and just and forgave our sins. He adopted us into his family, and we await a glorious future with him forever.

Others may think we are crazy and ask, "Why serve a God who does not pay better? Why serve a God who does not make you rich and give you a painless, healthy life?" Well, sometimes God does those things. But even when our lot in life seems no better than our enemies', God still gives us joy and satisfaction. Even if we live in daily pain, we will trust him. Why? Because we believe *in* him. We are betting our lives on him. With God, we are "all in." We have risked everything on his goodness because we know he loves us. After all, he sent his Son to die for us. This God-on-a-cross is worthy of our trust. Amazing love! How can it be?

PRAYER

I believe in you, Father.
You are *my* Father.
The Father of Jesus Christ
who is my brother.
You are Father of my family.
Our Father.
The family of God.

God the Father Almighty.
Above all,
in all,
through all,
able to do anything
but fail.

You care for me.
Provide for me.
Direct me.
And you love me.

I believe in God the Father Almighty.
The loving God.
The God.
The *only* God
Our God.
My God.
I believe.
Amen.

CREATOR

I have no idea why God
created the world. Maybe
God was bored and needed
something to watch.
—Scott

Why did God create the world? Was it to give himself something to watch, as Scott suggests? And how did God do it? Over the last fifty years, secularists and Christians have battled over the question of how the world came into being. The arguments have made both sides look foolish at times. However, Christians have always claimed that God is the creator. What exactly do we mean by this? And is it possible to be a Christian without being a creationist?

All Christians are creationists. We do not all agree on how creation happened, but we all believe God himself is the creator.

Christians simply reject the notion that creation "just happened" without God's involvement. We believe God made it happen. Sure, we debate among ourselves about exactly when and how, but we all agree on who and why—God the Father Almighty is the creator of heaven and earth.

THE CREATOR GOD

Our statement of faith in the creed is more about God than about creation. We do not say, "I believe in creation," but rather, "I believe *God* is the creator of heaven and earth." The God of the Old and New Testaments is the creator, and his creation gives us signs about what he is like. God brought everything into being. Nothing came into being on its own apart from God. To us, God is the First Cause, the Original Source of all creation.

We Christians are unbelievers when it comes to competing stories of creation. Certain beliefs rule out other beliefs, and our belief about God rules out some other beliefs. We do not believe that another god or some impersonal force is the real creator. We say creation is the work of the Father of Jesus Christ, the God of Abraham, Moses, and the Apostle Paul. We disbelieve accounts of creation that describe matter coming into being by purely natural causes. We do not believe that energy and matter have always existed or that it was through a series of natural events that the universe sprang into being as it is. We are hard to "convert" to these

40

competing belief systems. We are stubborn unbelievers because we believe what the creed affirms, which is what the Bible teaches—God is the creator of the heavens and the earth. We persist in believing this even in the face of high-pressure "evangelistic" tactics from devotees of competing creation accounts. Because we are believers in God, we are unbelievers in other, godless creeds.

Christians *believe* that God is the creator, though we cannot prove it beyond all doubt to those who disbelieve, any more than they can prove their accounts to us. No matter how much scientific data we marshal, we can seldom convince those who hold to another belief system. That doesn't matter to us. We believe in spite of the fact that others hold a different idea and even ridicule us for our faith. Christians have always done so.

We differ amongst ourselves, however, on exactly how active God was in creation. Some Christians believe he kept a distance and established the causal laws that produced the universe. Others see God active and near, creating by his very touch. Some believe this happened in seven literal days while others think it took millions of years, and there are a dozen views in between. Nevertheless, all Christians agree on this: God is the creator of the heavens and the earth. At all times and in all places, Christians have agreed that by whatever means it took place, God did it; God created the world.

We believe that a particular God is the creator, *our* God, *the* God, the *only* God. We are not speaking of some God-above-all-other-gods. That would make creation a sort of "court of the

41

Gentiles" where we gather with all other religions in more-or-less equal standing. No, to us the creator is God the Father Almighty. When we affirm that in the creed, we are speaking of one specific father—the Father of "Jesus Christ, His only Son, our Lord." Christ was not an afterthought, created along with everything else. Christ was "begotten not made." Christ was present at creation, so when we say God created, we mean that Christ was involved. To Christians, creation was not the work of some nameless above-all-other-religions deity; it was the work of the Holy Trinity—God the Father, Son, and Holy Spirit. Christians are Trinitarian creationists.

And there's more. We Christians believe the Son was an active participant in creation. He was not an onlooker. We believe that "by him all things were created: things in heaven and on earth, visible and invisible" (Col. 1:16). "In the beginning was the Word, and the Word was with God, and the Word was God. He was with God in the beginning. Through him all things were made; without him nothing was made that has been made" (John 1:1–3). To Christians creation is a Christian act—an act of Jesus Christ. The Christian answer to the question "Who created?" is "the Trinity." To insist that there is only one God and that that God is the sole agent responsible for creation may seem narrow-minded in an age when people place a high value on finding common ground with other religions. Nevertheless, this is what Christians everywhere at all times have believed: God is the creator, and Christ is God and therefore took part in the act of creation.

42

WHAT DID HE CREATE?

We believe God created everything, not just our own planet Earth. When many people hear the term *creationist*, they think primarily of human life and prepare themselves for a debate on the theory of evolution. The doctrine of creation, however, encompasses not just this planet but all planets and heavens combined. Certainly it is interesting to think about how our own planet got here, but the creation of this earth and the life it contains is not what Christians are talking about when we confess our faith in God as creator. We believe God created all matter everywhere—from tiny specks of material trillions of light years away to our own Earth and the flower outside our window. Moreover, we believe God created all energy too, and all so-called dark matter and everything else, even things we don't yet know about. If there are parallel universes, God created them too. We believe that if, as some say, everything sprang from a tiny, concentrated ball of energy, then God created that energy. If there is life somewhere else in these huge swirling galaxies, God created that life. God created it all. He is more than the totem god of one planet—he is the God of all.

There is more. God created microscopic matter too. We believe God made all the visible elements of the universe, and he also made the things you can't see, such as the microscopic specks nobody knew about until the invention of modern microscopes.

43

We believe God created electrons and neutrons and protons and photons and quarks and gluons and whatever other particles might be found and named in the future. We believe God made all matter and energy we might never see but only theorize about based on observing its effects. Seen and unseen, God made it all. Everything outside of God was created by God.

There is still more. God made the heavens as well as the earth. Ancient people conceived of the universe as having layers, with the earth below and the firmament above. Far above this, separated by a great ocean, were the heavens where God's throne existed. While our view of the universe may differ, we fully agree with the ancients that God created even "the heavens," meaning all nonmaterial worlds. Indeed, we believe there *is* an invisible, nonmaterial world that is not subject to human scientific discovery. God created that world—a domain that exists above us and beside us. Christians claim that the effects of this spiritual world can be felt in our own world. Atheist naturalists think we are nuts—they deny the existence of this nonmaterial world and claim when gazing into space, "There is nothing more than what we see." However, Christians believe in a spiritual world as well as a physical one. Christians believe God is the creator of both the seen and unseen worlds and any other worlds or dimensions we have not yet discovered. God is the creator of all.

HOW DID GOD CREATE?

Christians are not sure exactly how God created these things. Thinkers in our early church proposed various explanations for how God created matter and energy and space and time and life. Some saw creation as an *emanation*, an indirect effect of God, as light and heat are to a flame. Others saw creation as a *construction* made by God out of preexisting matter so that creation was the bringing of order from chaos. Still others saw God's creation as *artistry*, a work of beauty like that produced by a potter or songwriter, made for others to enjoy. A few early Christians even argued that an inferior being created the physical world because a good God could not dirty himself with material things, which they considered evil. However, it wasn't long before the vast majority of Christians came to agree that God created *ex nihilo*—out of nothing. Ever since that time, Christians everywhere have believed that while we may not know exactly how God created the universe, he did not build it out of preexisting materials but produced it out of nothing whatsoever. God spoke; creation happened.

Sure, we are curious about how it happened. Did God make our earth in six solar days back in 4004 B.C.? Did he create the whole universe at the same time? Did he create it slowly over millions of years? Did creation happen in a single moment eons ago with a "big bang"? Or did God arrange a series of big bangs and collapses in a row? Did God create in stages, first creating the universe, then planets, then plants and animals, and finally human beings? Is God still creating matter and energy today? How near or far was God from his creation acts? Did he establish the universe's natural laws in the beginning and by his will ordain how creation would occur over time? Or was God very near the act of creation, even present in the very atoms and electrons of the universe so that he is even now creating every living, growing thing?

Christian doctrine does not offer final answers to these questions. Individual Christians have hunches, theories, and opinions about these things, but none of us knows for sure. We read books on these ideas because we are curious, and some of us have even started organizations to promote one or another of these theories. However, we do not do this because we are Christian theologians. Christian theology says little about how God created. Theology addresses the "who" of creation—we believe the God of the Old and New Testaments and the Father of Jesus Christ our Lord is the creator of heaven and earth. How he created is interesting but is not relevant to our core faith. Christians insist on rejecting any theory of creation that leaves God out, but we are open to discussing any theory that confesses God as creator. We let Christians in the field of science give their theories on how it might have happened, but these scientific theories are merely interesting to us, not vital. We claim only that God is the creator.

46

WHY GOD CREATED

While Christian doctrine may be disinterested in the matter of how creation happened, it has much to say about why God created the world. God did not need stars or planets or antelopes or you and me to be complete. God is whole and complete in himself and needs nothing. That is the point of *ex nihilo* creation—creation out of nothing. God did not make the earth for his own entertainment, as Scott suggests in the opening quote. God has no need of entertainment. He does not need human beings because he is lonely or bored. There was perfect and complete love and fellowship in the Trinity itself long before creation. So why didn't God stick with the perfect world he already had? Why did God create?

God created out of love. Creation resulted from God's sheer fatherly kindness. God's love and goodness brought him to create energy and matter, birds, dogs, mountains, and you. God is love. God loves. God created. He chose to make you and everything else because of his love. He chose to make Mars and Earth, Adam and Eve, and you and me because he loves. Creation gives God more to love. Creation is a loving act of grace. It is a gift of God to you, to me, and to us. It is a miracle of love.

47

WHAT ABOUT US

What shall we say? God loved so much he created the world. He loved the world so much that he *entered* the world. Christ, the very Son of the God who created matter became matter himself, taking on the form of a human being and experiencing life on earth. The Creator became creation. This means that God's creative act and his act of redemption are inseparable. God first created the world then entered that world as a baby, born in Bethlehem of Judea on that starlit night. What wondrous love!

Creation is a gift from God. This is why we care for creation. The world is God's handiwork and it deserves our attention. When we lift up our eyes to the mountains or see a stunning sunset, what shall we do? We will praise God for his handiwork and we will be moved to care for it as if it were the masterpiece of a renowned painter. We are grateful. We rejoice. We praise. We love God in return—for he first loved us. In the rustling grass, we hear him pass. Yet we do not worship the grass but God, its maker.

As beautiful as creation is, we know the world is not God's Son—Jesus Christ is his Son. It is in Christ that we see the "best picture of God ever taken." We love creation, but we love the Son more. The beauty of creation causes us to turn our eyes upon Jesus and look into his face. It is in Jesus Christ that we live, move, and have our being. Creation is a miracle of love and grace, and it reminds us of the greater miracle: the miracle of love and grace by which God saved our souls. The rising sun prompts us to praise the Son that will never set.

PRAYER

I praise you, Creator of all things—
matter and energy,
planets and stars and universes,
mountains and lakes,
birds and flowers,
grass and trees,
and me.

You made it all, Lord.
By your hand.
By your Word.
All that I have
came from you.

Thank you for your gift of creation.
All because you loved.
I love you, Lord,
because you first loved me.
I believe in the creator of all.
I believe.
Amen.

50

JESUS CHRIST

> I think Jesus was the greatest man
> who ever lived. Of all human
> beings, he came closest to what God
> intended. He was just like us in that
> he, too, lived under God's rule. He
> admitted that he didn't know things
> that only God knows, and that he
> did what God told him to do. God
> saw how good he was and called
> him his son, which proves that we
> can be children of God too—if we
> live the way Jesus did.
> —Brett

It makes sense that Christians would have something good to say about Jesus Christ. Yet many people find it hard to believe that Jesus Christ could have been anything other than a human being, just like you and me. Brett speaks for many people who admire the life and teachings of Jesus Christ but aren't sure he was anything other than an exemplary human being. That sentiment echoes one of the early heresies of the church, a false idea that sometimes surfaces today.

What exactly do Christians believe about Jesus Christ? Was Jesus such a good man that he *became* God's Son? What do all

Christians everywhere mean when they say they believe in "Jesus Christ, his only Son our Lord?" This question takes us into the core section of the creed.

CHRIST THE CORE

Christians say that belief in God is not separate from belief in Jesus Christ. We believe Jesus *is* God. This second section of the creed is the linchpin for Christian theology, for it is about Jesus Christ. Here is where we differ from Islam and Judaism, which are also monotheistic religions that accept the idea of a creator. We, however, confess that Jesus Christ is God. Our God is tri-une—Father, Son, and Holy Spirit. We believe that Jesus was more than a very good man. We believe he is God.

Jesus

We believe in Jesus. Our word *Jesus* is based on the Greek form of the name Joshua (*Yeshua* in Hebrew), which means *savior*. The angel Gabriel announced this name for the child who would be born to Mary, when he said, "You shall call his name Jesus, for he will save his people from their sins." Jesus is our Savior. We are not saved by the idea of Jesus, meaning a set of beliefs that have been pronounced by this or that denomination. We are saved by the *person* Jesus Christ, who lived on earth and was crucified. We believe the person Jesus Christ is God. We Christians claim that Jesus is

God incarnate. He not merely was God but also is God, for he is alive today. It is not the case that we consider the Father to be the true God and Jesus Christ to be some sort of lesser god. We confess the full divinity of Jesus. He is *very God*, as the Nicene Creed puts it. Jesus is the name of a real person, Jesus of Nazareth who lived in a particular time and place on this earth. This real person called Jesus of Nazareth was, is, and forever will be God.

Christ

We believe Jesus is the Christ. The term *Christ* is not Jesus' surname; it's his title. We believe in Jesus, the Christ. Christ means *anointed one* or *messiah*. Christians believe the Father anointed Jesus by the Holy Spirit to be the promised Messiah. He is the King of the Jews, and he is also our King. He was spoken of in ancient times by the prophets, who foretold his coming. This Jesus who came in real time was the Messiah the Jewish people had been waiting for. He is prophet, priest, and king, and he fulfills the covenant God made with the ancient nation of Israel whereby it would bless all nations. Jesus is the Lord of Jews and Gentiles alike. Jesus is the Christ.

His Only Son

We believe Jesus Christ is God's only Son. The ancient Apostles' Creed says, "His only Son, our Lord," and that should have been enough to convince all Christians that Jesus is God.

Jesus Christ is God's Son; therefore, Jesus Christ is divine. That's that. However, early in our history, serious thinkers wondered about the relationship between the Son and the Father. Was the Son equal with the Father, or was there some hierarchy, some chain of command, within the Trinity? Maybe the Father was the real God, and the Son was some sort of lesser god. Or perhaps Jesus was just a man who had lived such a good life that God adopted him as a son. During the first three centuries of our history, Christians wondered about these things. They wondered if the Son of God might have been *created* by God like everything else and was therefore something less than God.

In the early days of the church, leaders gathered together in one place to decide questions like this. In A.D. 325, just a dozen years after the state-sponsored persecution of Christians ended, three hundred bishops gathered at Nicaea (in modern-day Turkey) to resolve the question of whether Jesus was fully God or was some lesser being. Arius, a popular pastor from Alexandria, Egypt, strung together a series of Bible references to defend the position that Jesus was *like* the Father but was *made* by the Father. Athanasius, also from Alexandria, pieced together other Bible references to argue that Jesus was not made at all but was of the same eternal *substance* as the Father. The debate continued for more than a month until a final vote was taken. The result was overwhelming. All but two bishops sided with Athanasius, and they formed the Nicene Creed to expound on what the church

54

meant when it said that Jesus is "His only Son, our Lord." By the year 381, the Nicene Creed had piled up a long list of terms to make it emphatically clear that Jesus is indeed God: "begotten of His Father before all worlds; God of God, Light of Light, very God of very God, begotten, not made, being of one substance with the Father by whom all things were made."

Thus the orthodox Christian belief holds that the Son of God existed from before all time and was begotten out of the Father, not made. Other religions, notably Islam, have since argued that the bishops at Nicaea made a mistake. They claim that Jesus was a great prophet, a good teacher, or the best example of humanity that ever existed—but he was not God. They demote Jesus and promote the Father. Christians have continually responded by insisting that Jesus is very God of very God, just as the Nicene Creed says.

Lord

We believe Jesus Christ, God's Son, is God and thus Lord. The very first creed was even simpler than the Apostles' Creed, containing just three words: "Jesus is Lord." That creed was penned by the apostle Paul, and it appears in Romans 10:9, 1 Corinthians 12:3, and Philippians 2:11. Our word *lord* is a translation of the Greek term *kyrios*, which is the same term used in the Greek version of the Old Testament to mean *Yahweh*, which is the name of God (see Ex. 3:14). Jesus is God.

In the Roman Empire, citizens were required to confess that Caesar was God, using the same term, *kyrios.* They would say, "Caesar is Lord." Understandably, Jews and Christians refused to obey this law. They would not offer incense to a statue of Caesar and recite the secular creed "Caesar is Lord." The Jews affirmed that only Yahweh is Lord, and the Christians insisted that Jesus is Lord. When we confess the creed, we claim that Jesus is God—the same God of the Old Testament—very God of very God. We are saying something more than that Jesus is *a* lord, as if he were the chief of some Christian manor. We say that Jesus is *the* Lord, the Lord God Jesus Christ.

This is no small claim in our day. The mood of our culture is to consider the deities of all religions to be equal. We feel pressure to admit, as ancient Roman citizens did, that some other being is "Lord" just as Jesus is. But we cannot bring ourselves to do it. Christianity would be far more acceptable today if we had adopted Arius's position and the beliefs that result from it. We could find common ground with other religions, share the same Father-God, and just have different prophets and ways to get to him. However, this has never been the position of Christian orthodoxy. We are not merely theists but Christians—we believe Christ is very God of very God. That may cause us to seem narrowminded when we appear on secular talk shows, but so be it. We Christians are Christ-ians. To us, Christ is God.

Our Lord

We believe Jesus Christ is God's Son our Lord. Yet because the Apostles' Creed was used as a baptismal creed, it begins with the pronoun *I*—I believe. The new believers stated their personal faith in Christ. Jesus is indeed my own personal Lord and Savior. However, he is also *our* Lord. The Nicene Creed begins with the pronoun *we* because it is intended to be a collective confession recited in worship. The Apostles' Creed implies this same community when it switches to first-person plural, saying, "our Lord." Jesus is the Head of the body of Christ, of which we are a part. We share one Lord, one faith, and one baptism. Jesus Christ is not some inner light we seek during quiet walks in our garden. He is the Lord of the church. He is *our* Lord—the Lord of all Christians everywhere. When we confess our faith in Jesus Christ as Lord, we simultaneously confess our place in the church. There are no lone-ranger Christians. Christians are a family, and we believe together.

THE REASON

Maybe all this sounds like theological gibberish. It might seem like an extravagant waste of time for the early church to have argued for more than a month over the nature of Jesus. What possible difference could it make that Jesus is "very God"? What does that have to do with me?

The Nicene Creed provides this answer: "who for us and for our salvation, came down from heaven." God became man for our salvation. God came to earth in Jesus *for us*. God was in Christ reconciling the world to himself. Why would God do this? He loved the world that much. We were hopeless in ourselves. Only he could rescue us. God was not obligated to do anything at all. Redemption is not an entitlement. God, in his great mercy, loved us so much that he became incarnate in Jesus Christ. He came down from heaven to rescue you and me and your neighbor and your children and your parents and all his enemies from their trespasses and sins. God knew human frailty. He knew weariness, hunger, and all of humanity's weaknesses. He experienced criticism, mocking, and betrayal. He knew temptation, trial, and pain. God incarnate faced opposition, suffering, and even death. Why would God do this? Because he loves.

WHAT ABOUT US

What shall we say? Others think we should loosen up on our insistence that Jesus is God. The world criticizes our view as narrow-minded and intolerant. Some urge us to demote Jesus to the status of just another human being—perhaps the greatest of all human beings, but a man nonetheless. They claim that Jesus is the stumbling block to religious unity. Why can't we just affirm Jesus was a great prophet and drop our God-talk about him? Couldn't we then come together with all other religions and accept the fact that there are many ways to the Father—the prophet Jesus being one of those ways? No, we cannot. Jesus Christ is very God.

We will not attempt to reverse the decision of Nicaea. Yes, we will talk with Jews and Muslims and Buddhists and Hindus. More, we will listen to them—for we can always learn from others. Most of all, we will love those of other religions, just as Jesus loves us. However, we will not leave *Jesus Christ our Lord* behind. If we did, we would no longer be Christians.

We love God because he first loved us. He loved the world so much that he sent his only begotten Son. It was first and last and always an act of supreme love. Divinity became humanity so that humanity might partake in divinity. It is too much for us to fathom. How could we respond to such wondrous love? What can we do to repay God for his unfathomable love? Nothing! There is no gift that would repay God's vast love. We are like the day laborer with a million-dollar debt. We can never repay it. Our service to God cannot repay him. Following his rules will not repay him. Loving our enemies and feeding the poor will not repay him. We should indeed do all these things, and we shall. Yet even if we did these things perfectly for our entire lives, it would still be a gift far too small. So what do we do? We marvel. We are astounded. Dumbfounded! We praise and worship him. What a great plan of salvation, "that God should love a sinner such as I." His love is greater than the highest hills and deeper than the deepest sea. There is nothing we can do to repay God's grace. We simply confess what we believe, with gratitude for his great love: "I believe in God the Father Almighty, Maker of heaven and earth; And in Jesus Christ, His only Son, our Lord."

PRAYER

I believe in you, Jesus Christ.
God's only Son.
Begotten of the Father
not made.
Son of God.
Our Lord.
My Lord.

I submit to you, Christ.
Be my Master.
Be my Lord.
I am clay, mold me.
I am dirty, cleanse me.
I am broken, mend me.
I am weak, strengthen me.
I have sinned, forgive me.

You, Lord, are my Lord.
You loved me and I love you in return.
I love.
I surrender.
I yield.
I believe.
I believe in Jesus Christ
God's only Son our Lord.
My Lord.
I believe.
Amen.

Who was conceived by the Holy Spirit,
born of the Virgin Mary. . . .
—Apostles' Creed

THE VIRGIN BIRTH

To tell you the truth, I've
always related more to Peter
or Paul than Jesus. They were
just average guys, like me.
Jesus was . . . well, Jesus was
God. He could do everything
right without a struggle. So
I sometimes ask the question
WWPD? What would
Peter do? That fits my style
better than asking what
Jesus would do.
—Zach

Christians say Jesus is God, but we also say he is a human being. So exactly how human is he? During his life on earth, did Jesus draw on power you and I don't have that enabled him to live a holy life? Is Zach right in thinking that Jesus was a ringer in the game of life? Was his victory over sin automatic because he is the Son of God? Zach's thought represents a common response to the two natures of Jesus, yet it is incorrect. The creed addresses the human nature of Jesus clearly in the phrase "conceived by the Holy Spirit, born of the Virgin Mary." After leading us to confess

Jesus as Lord, the creed shifts to the historical event behind that claim—the virgin birth.

How could a person be born without a human father? It cannot be. That has caused some people to conclude that the virgin birth is a legend or myth conjured up to communicate the idea that Jesus was a special man who told us something about God but that the stories about him do not accurately depict real-life events. Yet we Christians believe Jesus was actually born of a virgin. We affirm that Jesus' birth resulted from no action by any human father. How can this be? It was a miracle, an act of God that superseded the rules of nature as we understand them. It is among the mysteries and miracles of God. Jesus, a fully human being, was born of a woman who was a virgin.

The virgin birth has only a few Bible verses to support it, but it is critical to our doctrine. Theology is not a product of arithmetic, as if we could find out which subjects are most important by adding up the number of verses that mention them. Sometimes vital truths are found in only a few verses. Only Matthew and Luke directly mention the virgin birth, yet the creeds seize upon this truth, reminding us that it is critical to our faith. We Christians believe Jesus was born of the Virgin Mary. We do not know how it happened. We cannot fully explain it from a biological point of view. Yet we confess it as our belief every time we repeat the creed.

CONCEIVED BY THE HOLY SPIRIT

Why is it important to believe that Jesus was conceived by the Holy Spirit and not by Joseph or some Roman soldier on leave? Conception produced by a human father would clearly demonstrate Jesus' humanness, but it would lead to the conclusion that he is not "very God." Jesus is God. The virgin birth is a sign that Jesus is different than any person born before or after him. This was God becoming flesh—the incarnation. In this divine conception, God came down to us. When you and I were conceived, a new person was created—one who never existed before. However, Jesus Christ already existed *before* his conception. Jesus has existed from all eternity as a member of the Holy Trinity. At the conception of Christ, the Word of God was made flesh; God became human. We say, "Life begins at conception," when we oppose the practice of abortion, but in the case of Jesus it was not true—life existed before conception. Jesus became human when he was conceived, but he was already a person. The nativity is a sign to us that God drew near, but it is more than a sign—it was a real event that happened in real time on our planet. *God came down.* Thus, the good news of the gospel is not restricted to Calvary; it includes the nativity as well. We were lost and helpless, but God had pity on us and came down to save us. When we humans try to lift ourselves up, we usually fall. But in this case, Jesus Christ came down from heaven and was then raised up.

65

Jesus did not conceive himself, however. God the Son did not decide one day to join us on earth and reinvent himself as a human being. The Holy Spirit conceived him. In the conception we see the Holy Trinity. The Father sends, the Holy Spirit conceives, and the Son is born. The Holy Spirit is not the latecomer of the Trinity who showed up only at Pentecost; the Spirit is here at the conception of Christ, and has been present for all eternity. Later on, the Holy Spirit will come upon Jesus at his baptism (Luke 3:21) and will guide Jesus on earth (Luke 4:1) and will come upon the disciples at Pentecost (Acts 2). The Trinity has been constantly at work since before there was time, and no person of the Trinity works without the loving cooperation of the others. Jesus was "very God" when he was still the size of a grain of rice in Mary's womb.

How did the conception happen? We do not know. Conventional biology has always said it cannot happen. At least biology used to say this. As new reproductive technologies emerge, biologists are more humble about declaring what can and cannot happen. Some now can imagine a biologically reasonable (though highly improbable) explanation for virginal conception. Yet we Christians do not need biological explanations for the virgin birth in order to believe it. It is our confession of faith. We beleive it and always have. If it is someday proven or explained, fine, but we believe it now without explanation or proof. We do not believe these things because they have been reproduced in a double blind study. We believe these things because we are *Christian.* Wondering how such a thing could happen is okay. The Virgin Mary herself could not believe it. She simply accepted the words of Gabriel: "Nothing is impossible with God" (Luke 1:37). We accept this answer too. Christians believe some impossible things. Two of those impossibilities serve as bookends to Christ's earthly life—the virgin birth at the beginning and the resurrection at the end. We believe them both. We serve a God who makes impossibilities possible.

BORN OF THE VIRGIN MARY

The conception by the Holy Spirit tells us Jesus was fully God and at the same time fully human. That he was conceived by the Holy Spirit tells us he is God; that he was born of the Virgin Mary tells us he was human—two natures in one person. Jesus is God but he is not "only" God—he was human too. To elevate either side of his two natures is a theological error. God became a human being. This is the mystery of the incarnation. Jesus is the Son of God and is at the same time Jesus the Son of Man—God and man at once. From the lofty idea of being conceived of the Holy Spirit, we come to the lowly idea of full humanity. Jesus grew in Mary's womb from a speck to the size of a thumb and into a fully developed fetus. Jesus did not appear as a fully grown man. He started out like you and me—as a tiny embryo completely dependant on his mother's placenta for nourishment. What love! God loved us so much that he would submit to becoming

67

totally dependent on the workings of a mother's womb. Christ was equal with God, yet he became a tiny helpless dependent embryo—the *vulnerable God*. Jesus became a fetus, then a boy, then a teenager, and eventually an adult man with real human genes. He was fully human, not partially so. God's life as a human began with his first nine months in a womb. He took his first breath as a human at birth. He suckled at his mother's breast. He wore the first-century equivalent of diapers. He played as a child, lived as a teen, and worked as a carpenter when he grew up. He got tired and hungry and was lonely. He was tempted at all points as we are, yet was without sin. He lived a holy life. He did this as a human being. He beat the Devil on human turf.

In the opening quote, Zach is wrong—Jesus was every bit as human as Peter and Paul. The difference is Jesus did not sin, and Peter and Paul did. When we say, "Oh that was easy for Jesus—he was God," we are guilty of bad doctrine. Jesus took no shortcuts that are not available to you and to me today by God's grace. Jesus showed us the tremendous possibilities of humanity and holiness. Some complain, "I could believe in holiness if I ever saw it, but who lives the life of holiness?" We point to Jesus. The life of Jesus is a testimony to what we ought to be and what we can be—totally devoted followers of God. This is why Jesus is dismissed by people like Zach. We prefer sinner-models like Peter and Paul because they make it easier to excuse our failures. Yet Jesus never cheated when faced with temptation—he beat Satan as a human. "Born of the Virgin Mary" tells us Jesus was not just fully divine—he was fully human too.

MARY, MOTHER OF GOD

Beyond Jesus Christ there are two humans mentioned in the creed—Pontius Pilate and the Virgin Mary. These two nicely represent all of humanity. Pilate represents those who reject or dismiss Christ, while Mary represents believers who submit to him. Protestants cringe at the phrase "Mary, mother of God," but it is a core belief of Christians—Jesus is God and Mary was his mother. Mary was an ordinary girl who actually became the human mother of God incarnate. Jesus is God, and he was "born of a woman" (Gal. 4:4). Protestants rightly accuse Roman Catholics of taking Mariology to excess by extending her virginity perpetually and making her nearly a co-redemptrix with Christ. Yet Protestants err on the other side, dismissing her as a minor player in the story. The truth is Mary was a disciple of Jesus—the first disciple. She was his follower and was found among his traveling companions. She was present at the cross, and Mary was filled with the Holy Spirit at Pentecost along with the other leaders of the church (see Acts 1:12–14). Mary was a highly favored girl the Father chose to bear and raise his only begotten Son our Lord. Mary reminds us that Jesus Christ was not a ghost of God or a divine apparition, but was a real human being—the Word made *flesh*. Flesh like you and me.

69

VERY GOD AND VERY MAN

Jesus was both God and man—a 200 percent person. Christians see here the wonderful mystery of the incarnation—God in human flesh. We do not favor Christ's divinity at the expense of humanity, nor do we favor his humanity at the expense of his divinity. Jesus was equally born of the Holy Spirit *and* the Virgin Mary. The wording of earliest creeds actually said it that way. Christ is both divinity and humanity at once in perfect union. In the early years of church history, numerous ideas arose explaining the nature of Jesus as we tried to sort out what the Bible meant. The debate continued for years to solve the riddle of Christ's two natures. *Photinus* argued that Jesus the man lived such a good life that he earned the right to become the Son of God. *Manicheus* proposed that Jesus did not have real flesh but only appeared to be human. The *Ebionites* suggested that Jesus was conceived of male sperm. *Valentinus* postulated that the Holy Spirit put a heavenly creature inside Mary's womb so that Mary contributed nothing but was merely a human incubator. *Apollinarius* suggested that Jesus did not have a soul, and *Eutyches* saw the nature of Jesus as a co-mingling of divinity and humanity—a Jesus who was part human and part God. *Nestorius* argued that God merely indwelled a human container but was not fully human himself. None of these ideas prevailed. Today we label these notions "heresy," but these aberrant doctrines actually helped the early church clarify its own doctrine based on the Bible. In 451, the Council of Chalcedon hammered out the wording Christians have accepted ever since. Jesus was both human and divine at once, both very God and very man at the same time. Any time we emphasize one at the expense of the other we are headed into error.

WHAT ABOUT US

What shall we say? How will we respond to the incarnation? God made flesh. We have a God who was acquainted with sorrow. He understands our pain. God became human and lived among us. He got weary like we do. He knew opposition, betrayal, and grief as we do. He faced rejection, death, and burial like us. Why? Why would God do this? He did it for us. The Word became flesh "for us and for our salvation," as the Nicene Creed states it. He did not do it for himself but for us. The Christmas bumper sticker "Jesus is the reason for the season" is true in one way. However, in another way it falls short. The reason for the season is *us*. Christmas is not some sort of celestial pageant play put on for the Father's entertainment. It is the ultimate act of love and grace done "for us and for our salvation." God made flesh. Christmas is about God showing pity on our poor estate and intervening. It is God himself showing up in person entering human life. The incarnation is God's ultimate Christmas gift.

Others mock the virgin birth. They challenge us to prove it or explain it. However, the evidence we offer does not convince them. We do not try to prove the virgin birth—we confess it for the entire world to hear and believe or reject. We pronounce our faith in God. We worship the God of possible impossibilities. Some refuse to believe, but we do not let their unbelief shake our belief. Instead, we believe and let our belief challenge their unbelief. God really did become human. This God-become-human lived a human life, yet without sin. This very man went to the cross and died in our place. He became the supreme sacrifice for our sin. We had nothing to do with it. We could not save ourselves. Jesus paid it all. So we believe. We do not understand it. God become human to die for us. Can this be? For *us*? For *me*? What can we say? We join Mary in her response to the angel's announcement: "Let it be unto me as you have said." God, be merciful to me a sinner. What wondrous love.

72

PRAYER

How can this be?
Born of a virgin.
I don't know how,
but I believe.
Mary's child,
fully God,
fully human,
God's own Son.

The Lord and Master.
Human like me.
Born like me.
A baby like me.
A child like me.
Weary like me.
Criticized like me.
Tempted to sin like me.
Yet without sin.

I praise your faithfulness, Christ.
Very God and very human,
Jesus Christ our Lord.
Jesus Christ *my* Lord.
A loving God with a loving Son.
It is more can I can comprehend.
Yet it is true.
I believe.
Amen.

Who . . . suffered under Pontius Pilate, was crucified, dead, and buried. He descended into hell.
—Apostles' Creed

THE SUFFERING, DEATH, AND BURIAL OF JESUS CHRIST

> God wants your success more than anything else. He wants you to be richer and healthier and happier than those in the world. His plan is to prosper you so you don't ever experience pain, suffering, or poverty. This is why Christ died—it is the good news of the gospel.
> —Televangelist

The cross screams "Liar! Liar!" at the prosperity gospel that is so popular today. A prosperity preacher told one of my college professors, "God owns the cattle on a thousand hills—he wants you to have whatever you want, including a new Cadillac. God gives these things to his children."

She replied, "That's odd—he gave his Son a cross."

The TV preacher quoted above stated a partial truth: God does give good gifts to his children. But sometimes that gift involves a cross, as it did for Jesus Christ, his only Son our Lord.

The Apostles' Creed leaps from God's incarnation to the passion and death of Jesus Christ. We are swept from the happy story of a tiny baby's birth to the painful story of a grown man's suffering and death. We move from Christmas to Good Friday in just a few words. Jesus died. Believers and unbelievers alike agree on this part of the creed. Jesus really lived as a first-century man, was crucified as a criminal, died, and was buried—this is historically uncontroversial. Both Christians and atheists agree on this part of the creed. No well-informed person can deny the existence and death of Jesus. Where we differ is in what his death means. To some, Christ's death was the end of a failed or false messianic hope. To Christians it is the triumphal accomplishment brought by obedience to his mission. The Son of God became a human being precisely in order to die.

SUFFERED UNDER PONTIUS PILATE

Why does the creed leave out the great moral teachings of Jesus and the intriguing stories about him by jumping from the incarnation to crucifixion? Where are the Beatitudes and parables and the familiar accounts of healing blind men and walking on water? Here it helps to remember that the creed does not replace the Bible but underscores its vital doctrines. Without the death and resurrection, the teachings of Jesus are nothing more than great moral lessons from a first-century rabbi.

Some reject the divinity of Jesus while celebrating his moral teachings. Christians will not do this. We argue that Jesus was more than a great moral teacher. He was "very God" who became a man and suffered and died for our sins. Jesus did not come just to teach us how to live. He came to die for our sins and redeem us. He was obedient unto death—even death on the cross. Whenever we get preoccupied with the teachings of Jesus to the exclusion of his nature and mission, we start to wander away from the true gospel.

However, the creed does detail the whole life of Jesus. This section describes the humiliation of the Son of God—his coming down from heaven and identifying with the human condition. His life on earth was not one of triumph and success in the way we usually understand those terms. His life was one of suffering and affliction. The Son, who knew all the glory of heaven, took on human form and suffered enough. Jesus was raised in a poor family and was acquainted with grief, even losing his earthly father to death. The Son of God knew hunger and thirst, opposition, betrayal, and rejection. The entire life of Jesus Christ was a life of suffering that climaxed in his suffering under Pontius Pilate.

How did Pontius Pilate, a Roman governor of Judea, get into our creed? It seems odd. It does root the story in history; but just think, every week for more than two thousand years, Christians have recalled the name of this flimsy government functionary. Was his wife's dream a premonition of this shameful recollection throughout the ages (see Matt. 27:19)?

THE SUFFERING, DEATH, AND BURIAL OF JESUS CHRIST

With Pilate, politics intrudes into the story. It reminds us that Jesus was crucified legally by the imperial government of his day. This may serve to remind us that we should have a healthy suspicion of state power. We are sometimes tempted to use state power to do evangelistic work for us, but every time that has happened in history it has brought more negative than positive for God's kingdom. Some Muslims are comfortable establishing religious empires, but serious Christians are wary of imperial power. One might be able to become a Muslim by force of law, but only spiritual birth can make one a Christian.

The inclusion of Pilate's name reminds us that we are speaking here of a real event, fixed in historical time under real historical figures. What we believe about Jesus is not made up. It is an actual event and not a fable.

The Son of God suffered. Our word *passion* comes from the Greek word for suffering. Today we elevate the word *passion* to mean fervor and enthusiasm rather than suffering. We like the idea of passion, but we are keener on its meaning as zeal than as suffering. God's Son experienced passion of the suffering kind. Christians have faced suffering and death differently ever since. The passion of Christ should have lain to rest forever the success or prosperity "gospel" of the gospel-less televangelist quoted at the beginning of this chapter. The good news of the gospel is not about wealth, health, and success. The good news is that Jesus Christ became the perfect sacrifice for our sins. People would rather hear about success than sin, but the true gospel is about deliverance from sin.

The central act of Jesus Christ was not walking on the water or making a blind person see—it was suffering death on Calvary. Jesus was sent to seek and to save those who are lost. The cross is central to our faith even though it may not sell very well to self-absorbed moderns seeking a boost for their career paths. While we do not glorify suffering or seek martyrdom on purpose, God's full participation in the human condition teaches us how to suffer when it becomes our portion. Jesus said, "Blessed are those who mourn" and "blessed are those who are persecuted" (Matt. 5). He was his own best object lesson.

WAS CRUCIFIED

Jesus did not die a natural death. He was killed by a most agonizing method, even by the standards of the brutal first century. He was crucified on a cross, a punishment that was reserved for criminals, slaves, and enemies of the state. On the cross, criminals were tortured to death. Offenders hung naked for hours with nails piercing their feet and hands. As they slumped, under the weight of their own bodies, they died from slow asphyxiation. This form of capital punishment was a sobering sight for the public and was done as a warning to potential lawbreakers. It was a public execution that took hours or even days, unlike the swift death brought by beheading or hanging. Jesus hung on the cross for hours, experiencing this slow, humiliating death. Nevertheless, he did so willingly. Christians do not see the death of Jesus as a story of mistaken injustice. It was the self-donation of the Son of God. He did this for us and our salvation. For our sake the one who did not know sin became sin (see 2 Cor. 5:21). The Son of God could have called ten thousand angels and been delivered from his predicament in an instant. Yet he was obedient unto death—even the death of the cross. He was smitten for our transgressions. He did it out of love.

On the cross, Christ gave us the supreme example of all the virtues he taught. Thomas Aquinas reminded Christians that on the cross we witness all the virtues of Christ wrapped up in one event. Here we see the highest love, for no one has greater love than to lay down his life for a friend. On the cross, we see humility, for he humbled himself and became obedient to this death. We see forgiveness even to the extent of his praying "Father forgive them" for the ones executing him. On the cross, we see patience, tenderness, compassion, and all the other virtues he taught us. On the cross Christ's teachings converge. To Christians, the cross is not just a story of evil men doing a bad deed. It is a story of a good man doing a good deed.

The world believes we are mad to think this way, but Christians are not ashamed of the cross. In the cross of Christ, we glory. The cross is central to how we see life. It is our central symbol. We pray

80

that God will draw us nearer to it. Pilate thought he got rid of Jesus, and Rome thought it had triumphed. However, we Christians know Pilate merely played a bit part in God's great story of redemption. It was not Rome but Christ who triumphed.

DIED AND WAS BURIED

The cross led to Christ's death and burial. Jesus suffered, died, and then was buried. He identified not only with human suffering but also with death. When they took Christ's body from the cross, it was dead. Some have imagined he only passed out and later woke up in the tomb. Muslims say he only appeared to die. But Christians confess in our creed that Jesus died—became completely void of life. They buried him. Why did Jesus have to die? He died for our redemption. He died in our place. He died so that he might fully identify with humanity. You and I will someday face our own burial. We all end up in a casket lowered into the ground or have our ashes scattered to the winds. When we Christians approach the time of our own death and burial, we do so with the knowledge that the Son of God faced burial before us. Christ gives us hope at the graveside. This is why we enter the doorway of death believing and not despairing. Christ's death supplies Christian martyrs with courage to face their own premature (and voluntary) deaths. Christ's obedience gives us a model to follow. His example shows us that death is temporary and not to be feared.

He died out of love for the whole world—and for you and for me. His faith in his own resurrection allowed him to go as a lamb to the slaughter. This is why we Christians face death differently than unbelievers do. We enter the dark doorway of death with faith and hope and love—for the doorway leads to light.

HE DESCENDED INTO HELL

Did Jesus go to hell? More than any other phrase in the Apostles' Creed, the statement that Jesus descended into hell baffles us. It is important to understand the term *hell*. The Hebrew word *sheol* (or grave) referred to a shadowy underworld people were assumed to inhabit after death. There they continued a ghost-like existence. The word *hades* is the Greek equivalent to *sheol*. Originally, the creed merely meant only this—Jesus descended to the place of the dead. Some modern editions of the creed say exactly this to avoid confusion: "He descended to the dead." Thus, when we say Christ descended into hell, we mean that he experienced death fully and completely—he entered the land of the dead.

Later in history, the phrase "descended into hell" came to mean more than was originally intended. There is yet another term used during New Testament times to designate the after-death— *gehenna*. Gehenna was thought to be a place of smoldering fire and brimstone, named after the smoking garbage dump in the ravine outside Jerusalem. This notion of the after-death place conjured the image of a place of punishment and separation from God, which is what we now think of when we use the word *hell*. Over the centuries, some Christian thinkers came to believe the creed meant that Jesus descended into the actual residence of Satan, defeating the Devil on his home turf. Christ "led captivity captive" (Eph. 4:8 KJV). These Christian thinkers did not dream up this idea on their own but based it on the Bible. One verse in 1 Peter was particularly important to this way of thinking: "For this is the reason the gospel was preached even to those who are now dead, so that they might be judged according to men in regard to the body, but live according to God in regard to the spirit" (1 Pet. 4:6).

From 1 Peter 4:6 (and other verses) came the idea of the "harrowing of hell." Many classic artworks of the Middle Ages vividly picture this, depicting Christ on Holy Saturday as entering the dungeons of the Devil and releasing from death those people who, by faith, had served God long before Christ came—Abraham, Isaac, Jacob, Joseph, Moses, and all the true followers of God from ancient times. By this thinking, even these people had the opportunity to hear the gospel when Christ preached to them in the place of the dead, and they responded by faith. So even people who lived in the time before Christ were not saved by their own good works but by faith alone when they faced Christ on Holy Saturday. In the triumphant harrowing of hell, Christ defeated Satan and bound him so that even now he is limited in his work. Satan is an already-defeated foe who enjoys a bit of freedom for the time being. The final battle between good and evil will be merely an echo of the battle already won by Christ on Holy Saturday.

Whichever interpretation Christians choose to accept—the early or the later one—we know that Christ was not *sent* to death or hell kicking and screaming. He went out of love. Christ fully laid down his life for us. Whether he entered the Devil's house and bound Satan at that time or not, we do not know for sure. What we do know is that Satan is a defeated foe and our Lord is the triumphant Victor.

WHAT ABOUT US

What shall we say? How shall we respond when surveying the wondrous cross? Our God became flesh and died. What kind of a religion is this? It is *our* kind of religion. At the center of a Christian's faith is a story of God's Son, who died willingly for our sins. God had pity on our helpless estate because he loved the world. We were sinners with no hope of recovery. Yet God sent his Son, who freely gave himself as the ransom for all. Jesus paid it all. He was the sacrifice to end all sacrifices. Our Lord is the perfect Lamb of God who takes away the sins of the world. Such love, such wondrous love! This is why Christians place crosses in front of our churches and put them on the top of steeples.

Sure, we Christians face suffering and death along with unbelievers. Yet we face these things differently because we know God turned the apparent defeat of Good Friday into the glorious victory of Easter Sunday. We know God does not desert us when we die. Throughout our history we Christians have been persecuted, oppressed, tortured, and martyred by being fed to lions or burned at the stake. Yet we do not deny our faith, because we know this life is a vapor that vanishes away like morning dew. Life is short but eternal life is forever. One day we will rise again. You cannot truly kill a person who has eternal life. Yes, we value life; but we do not cling to it as unbelievers do. We value life but we value eternal life more. You can kill us, but only temporarily. We have hope because the Christ we worship and adore was tortured, killed, and buried long before we were born. We are willing to become like him in his death if that is our calling. Therefore, if you insist that we deny Christ and threaten us with death, we will defy your paltry threats. You cannot truly kill us, for we already have eternal life. Because the Firstborn of all Creation is also the Firstborn from the Dead. Christ arose, and so shall we.

85

PRAYER

You died for me, Christ.

For sins of the whole world.

For *my* sins.

What can I say?

Thank you, Father, for loving the world,

for sending your Son.

Thank you, Jesus, for your faithfulness

unto death.

Even death on a cross.

You loved and it cost you your life.

A perfect sacrifice.

You knew no sin

yet became sin.

For us all.

For *me*.

Christ, you are the Savior of the world.

You are our Savior.

You are *my* Savior.

I confess.

I repent.

I trust.

I believe.

Amen.

86

The third day he arose again from the dead; he ascended into heaven, and sits at the right hand of God the Father Almighty.
—Apostles' Creed

THE RESURRECTION
AND ASCENSION OF JESUS

I understand it like this: when Jesus' body was killed, the God part of him left his body and became a spirit that appeared to the disciples, sort of like a ghost. About forty days later, this God part of Jesus went back to heaven.

—Cathy

Cathy is not alone in her mistaken belief. In today's church, it is not uncommon for people to reject the physical resurrection of Jesus and opt for a spiritual one instead. They do not embrace this heresy purposefully but usually do it unthinkingly. If questioned, Cathy would probably not say that Jesus' body continued to rot in the grave while his "ghost" arose. Yet without giving the matter careful thought, she might begin to think this way. Lots of people do.

Gaining understanding and clarity on this doctrine is important because the resurrection of Jesus is the template for our own future resurrection. If the body of Jesus was raised, then we can expect our own bodies to be raised too. If only his spirit was raised while his body rotted away, then we should expect only a spiritual resurrection for ourselves in the future. Christians have always said that the actual body of Jesus was raised. Christians have consistently rejected the idea of a spiritual-only resurrection as a heresy—a belief that simply is not true.

TWO TYPES OF UNBELIEVERS

The death and burial of Jesus is widely accepted by all serious students of history, believers and unbelievers alike. Disagreement arises, however, regarding his resurrection and ascension. There are two kinds of unbelievers at this point in the creed. The first group treats the resurrection as a tall tale made up by early Christians after their hoped for Messiah disappointed them. This group views the resurrection story as a sort of plan B. To them, Jesus had failed in his messianic mission and these stories were invented to keep the Jesus movement going in the face of its failure. This first group dismisses the resurrection as a whacky story along the lines of UFO sightings and alien abductions.

A second group of unbelievers treats the resurrection as a meaningful myth created to say "something important" about Jesus—to show that he was a "special message from God." To them, the resurrection story is important, but not a historical event.

The first group of unbelievers is found in the world. The second group is sometimes found in the church. The second group may appear to be Christians in most ways, even basing their highly moral lifestyle on the ethical teachings of Jesus. But they are unbelievers when it comes to the historical resurrection of Jesus Christ.

We creedal Christians are a third group—*believers*. We believe that on the third day, Christ rose from the dead, and that for forty days he appeared to others, then ascended into heaven. We believe this really happened. To Christians, the resurrection is not a parable or a spiritual story, like one of Aesop's fables. To us this is a real event that took place in real time right here on earth on that first Easter morning. We do not celebrate the resurrection on Easter alone. We meet together on the first day of every week to recall this event. Each Sunday service is a mini-Easter at which we remember Christ's resurrection. Just as he rose on that first day, we, too, will rise someday.

THE THIRD DAY HE ROSE AGAIN

Jesus rose again on the third day. Before any of the four Gospels were widely circulated, the apostle Paul put it clearly: "He was raised on the third day according to the Scriptures" (1 Cor. 15:4). Jesus was crucified on Friday, the day before the Sabbath. He continued among the dead all day the second day, Holy Saturday.

However, on the third day—the first day of the week, Sunday—he arose and appeared to many of his disciples during the following forty days. Christians believe this actually happened; skeptics cannot bring themselves to accept it. They theorize that wild dogs must have devoured the corpse or the disciples themselves came and stole it. The worldview of a skeptic does not allow for miracles, so they find this greatest-of-all-miracles simply ridiculous. Thomas Jefferson went so far as to create a Bible that omitted all miracles— including the resurrection. Such a Bible, in the end, leaves only the great moral lessons of Jesus—and a dead body. But our Christian story does not end in death. It goes on with hope. We believe that on the third day, Christ arose and is still today the *living* Christ.

The resurrection of Christ is unique for that reason—Jesus is still alive. Others came back to life in Bible times, including Lazarus, a widow's son, and the daughter of a synagogue ruler; but they all died again later. For them, coming back to life merely delayed death, it was not a victory over it. The resurrection of Jesus was not a postponement; it was permanent. It was not resuscitation but resurrection. Jesus is alive. He is the firstfruits of the future resurrection that will include many more people. The body of Jesus that was moldering in the grave was resurrected, and he walked and talked with his disciples and eventually ascended into heaven. This gives us hope.

Who raised Jesus from the dead? The creed says, "He arose," suggesting that Christ raised himself from the dead. As he had willingly given himself over to death, so he chose to take back his

90

human body and rise in power and victory. However, this is only one way of putting it. We also often say that the Father raised the Son from the dead. Which is it? The Bible suggests both (see Matt. 16:21; Mark 8:31; Rom. 4:24; 1 Thess. 4:14). But there is more to consider. How does the Father work on earth? By the Holy Spirit. The Holy Spirit is the executive agent of the Father and Son. Thus, when the Father raised the Son, it would have been by the Holy Spirit, so we have all three members of the Trinity involved in the miracle of miracles. The resurrection of the Son was brought about by the Father, Son, and the Holy Spirit.

Why do we need a resurrection? Why would the story need to end this way? Is the resurrection so crucial? Wouldn't it have been good enough for Jesus to have "put his shoulder to the wheel of history, and, moving, it crushed him" as Albert Schweitzer saw the story ending? If we followed Schweitzer's way of thinking, we would base our lives on the great moral teachings of Jesus and then go to our death knowing we had lived a most fulfilling life, but we would have no hope of anything more. That is not the way we tell the story. It is not the way the Bible tells it either. Christians say Jesus is God who came down for us and our salvation. He came down as far as humans can go, unto death. Death could not hold him, and he rose again. The resurrection is the central miracle for Christians because it gives hope and meaning to our lives rather than simply showing the best way to cope with a miserable existence.

Christians might argue about the way creation happened—whether in seven days or over a longer period. We also debate the extent to which natural causes contributed to various healings in the Bible. But we do not argue about the resurrection. We believe it really happened. All Christians at all times and in all places have believed this. That does not mean we understand it or can prove it to others. We *believe* it. We may experience doubt about it at times, but when we repeat the creed, we remember what Christians have always believed—Christ is risen. In saying the creed, those with stronger faith uplift those with weaker faith. Together the church proclaims to the world (and to itself) that Christ rose from the dead.

Some in the apostle Paul's day doubted the resurrection. Paul penned strong words to the church at Corinth, where some of these doubters attended. What would we lose if there were no resurrection or if a "spiritual resurrection" had already happened? Paul warned that our proclamation would be empty, our faith would be foolish and vain, we would still be in our sins, our loved ones who died in the faith would have perished, and we would be a pitiable people (see 1 Cor. 15:13–19). If there is no resurrection, the gospel is a lie and we are gullible fools. This is precisely what skeptics say of us. They say we believe a lie and are a deluded. "People can't come back to life," they say. "It's impossible." We reply, "With God all things are possible."

What if archeologists found the bones of Jesus in Jerusalem and scientists were able to prove beyond all doubt that it really was the skeleton of Jesus Christ? That isn't going to happen, of course, but just imagine that it did. If we knew for sure that Jesus' body was not raised, what would we do? Some people would say, "It doesn't matter what they find." But for Christians it would matter. We make claims to ourselves about real events that happened in real time. Jesus Christ is not the Easter bunny—he is a real person who was really and truly raised from the dead. If it were finally proven that that belief were false, we would have to honestly reconsider our faith. If we continued as believers, we would need to create a new religion around a great teacher who wound up dead—just like everybody else. But we will not have to do that, for he is alive.

Christians do not believe the resurrection was merely a spiritual event either. We do not believe that the ghost of Jesus appeared to the disciples and then went back to heaven while his body rotted in the grave. We may be tempted to believe that because of the inadequate way we understand our own future resurrection, as we shall see later. We sometimes imagine that after we die, our spirit goes to be with God while our body lies in the ground forever. This is a sub-Christian belief, a pagan one. Christians believe that resurrection is not merely spiritual but also physical. The actual body of Christ was physically raised and went to heaven. The tomb was empty after the resurrection.

WITNESSES TO THE RESURRECTION

That we cannot prove the resurrection to an unbeliever does not mean that we have no proof whatsoever. We do not believe in the resurrection because "it just feels right"; we have evidence to support the claim. While it is not possible to empirically prove that the resurrection took place anymore than it is possible to empirically prove any historical event, we do have witnesses. The apostle Paul did not tell the doubting Corinthians they should believe just because they would look silly if they quit. On that basis alone, we would all still believe in Santa Claus. Instead, Paul offered the doubting church a solid list of eyewitnesses who had seen Jesus alive after his crucifixion. Paul told the Corinthians of Christ's appearances to Peter, the Twelve, a group of five hundred people at one time, James, all the apostles, and finally to himself. Even this list is incomplete, since Paul over-looked the other women at the tomb and Cleopas.

In addition to the eyewitnesses, there was the empty tomb, seen on Easter morning by a group of women, along with Peter and John. The foes of Jesus saw it, too, and bribed the guards to claim someone stole the body. However, even the empty tomb is not enough for a thinking person. There are ways a body could have been snatched, in spite of the presence of armed guards. When the empty-tomb reports came to the disciples, they were incredulous. They had to be convinced too, and Jesus appeared to them personally to make his resurrection known. Countless witnesses testified to seeing the resurrected Christ alive. If they all lied, they lied together, and many went to their death refusing to deny what they had seen. Would they have died for a lie? No, it really happened.

When people say, "I do not believe it," we cannot convince them. All we can do is urge them to get under the influence of the church so they may find faith. In the church we continue the apostles' witness to the resurrection by proclaiming it and praying to the living Christ. We know it is true. Some Christians say they decided to believe, and others say they got faith as a direct gift from God. Some of us came to faith slowly and others in a moment, like the apostle Paul. Yet we all eventually came to this belief: we serve a *risen* Savior. He lives!

HE ASCENDED INTO HEAVEN

After forty days on earth, Jesus returned in triumph to heaven, the starting point of his mission. He had accomplished his mission, been 100 percent obedient to the Father, lived a sinless life in human flesh, and defeated death and sin. He stooped so low as to experience death, and then he was raised so high as to return to the right hand of the Father Almighty at the time of his ascension.

Many Christians do not give much thought to the ascension. Perhaps it is because the fortieth day after the resurrection is a

95

Thursday and not a Sunday. We are better at celebrating Bible events that occur on Sunday. Many American churches simply ignore Ascension Day and focus on the secular holidays of the season—Mother's Day and Memorial Day. Yet the ascension is an important doctrine. At the very least, the ascension tells us that Jesus is not still walking the earth in bodily form. However, the more important implication of the ascension is theological: the resurrected human body of Jesus ascended *into heaven*. Just think: the first human body is already in heaven—the body of Jesus Christ. In the final resurrection, our bodies will simply follow the path Christ has already taken. Our own resurrected human bodies go to heaven too. We know this because that is precisely what happened to Christ's body. When Christ ascended, he did not leave his resurrected body on the Mount of Olives. He took his flesh and bones with him. He ascended physically. There is no need for a stone to be rolled away for a mere spirit to leave the tomb. Christ rose bodily and ascended likewise.

A human body sits right now at God's right hand. Just think of it. The Trinity does not have to go far to see an example of humanity. An example of humanness is there at the Father's right hand, Jesus Christ—very God and very man. In the incarnation and crucifixion, we see the humiliation of the divine. In the resurrection and ascension, we see the exaltation of humanity. Jesus Christ bore humanity into heaven. He is both the Son of God and the Son of Man *today*—very God and very man returned to heaven. He did not leave his "human part" behind when he rose. God-and-man returned to heaven as God-and-man. He is fully God and fully man right now. This is why we look to Christ as our representative. We do not have a high priest that is unacquainted with humanity. He does not just remember being human—he is human even now, just as he fully God. To Christians the ascension is comforting. It is an example and gives us hope as we look toward our own resurrection. Then we, too, will be with God forever. Christ bore humanity into heaven and now awaits the rest of humanity. We will join him there later.

HE SITS AT THE RIGHT HAND
OF GOD THE FATHER ALMIGHTY

Jesus sits beside God now. At this point in the creed, there is a surprising shift in tenses. So far, the past perfect tense has been used when speaking of Jesus: he was begotten, conceived, born, suffered, crucified, died, buried, and rose. Now the creed shifts to present tense, he *sits* at the right hand of God the Father Almighty. Thus, we do not follow a religion stuck in the past but one that speaks also of present and future. Our story is ongoing. Our quest is not for the historical Jesus but for the living and coming Jesus. We serve a risen Savior who is alive today. He will be here tomorrow too. After Christ completed his mission of coming down, he was elevated to the highest place, the right hand of God the Father Almighty. He

97

was enthroned and glorified, and his name is exalted above every other name. The creed reflects the words of Mark: "After the Lord Jesus had spoken to them, he was taken up into heaven and he sat at the right hand of God" (Mark 16:19). However, Mark and the creed both echo Psalm 110:1: "The LORD says to my Lord: 'Sit at my right hand until I make your enemies a footstool for your feet.'" Christ was exalted. Christ had already said so. When he gave the Great Commission, Jesus said, "All authority in heaven and on earth has been given to me" (Matt. 28:18). When he took his place at the side of the Father, he was taking a place of authority that was already his.

The right hand of God is the place of honor and authority. It is not as if the Holy Spirit is at the left hand, however. Augustine observed long ago that there are no left-hand spots in heaven. Christ is not passively sitting as if he is resting up in some celestial recliner after his earthly mission; he is active in heaven. Stephen made that clear in his vision: "But Stephen, full of the Holy Spirit, looked up to heaven and saw the glory of God, and Jesus *standing* at the right hand of God" (Acts 7:55, emphasis added). John pictured Christ on horseback in Revelation (19:11–16). So "sitting" can better be understood as dwelling. Christ dwells at the right hand of the Father.

What is Christ doing at God's right hand? He is interceding on our behalf. Jesus the God-man intercedes for us men and women: "because Jesus lives forever, he has a permanent priesthood.

Therefore, he is able to save completely those who come to God through him, because he always lives to intercede for them" (Heb. 7:24–25). He is a permanent and sympathetic high priest constantly interceding for us. As John put it, "we have one who speaks to the Father in our defense—Jesus Christ, the Righteous One" (1 John 2:1). We have a powerful friend in high places. He is our go-between. The Father shares his full authority with the Son. It will be Jesus Christ who comes to judge the living and the dead. However, we do not fear this coming judgment. We will not be condemned, for we have believed in his name and we trust in his atonement for our sins.

The way up is down. The Son of God who was equal with God humbled himself and came down to earth to die a painful death. It was as low as he could go. The Father "exalted him to the highest place and gave him the name that is above every name, that at the name of Jesus every knee should bow" (Phil. 2:9–10). We have an advocate right at the throne of heaven. He understands humanity completely. "For we do not have a high priest who is unable to sympathize with our weaknesses, but we have one who has been tempted in every way, just as we are—yet was without sin" (Heb. 4:15). Jesus Christ, our advocate, knows human frailty and human possibilities, for he was—and still is—both divine and human. What a mighty God we serve! Worthy is the Lamb that was slain.

WHAT ABOUT US

What shall we say? How can we respond to the resurrection and exaltation of Jesus Christ? We live triumphantly because, as Martin Luther put it, "Jesus has swallowed up and devoured death." Death remains, but it has lost its sting; Christ has pulled death's stinger out—all that remains is buzz. Christ died for us, and he also rose for us. He became the firstfruits of our own hope. For us and our salvation, he came down; and for us and our salvation, he went back up. God did it all for us out of his boundless love.

The resurrection changed everything. It is the turning point in the history of the universe. After the resurrection, a new world began. New wine began to flow. That event is God's pledge for our future. The war is won; the victory is complete. Skirmishes between life and death still occur, as if the foes of Christ have not yet heard that their master was defeated. But it is finished. Death, sin, and hell are defeated. Christ, the second Adam, has triumphed. The Son of Man who is also the Son of God is now in heaven interceding for us.

This is the good news of the gospel—God has said yes to humans. Christ now has all authority in heaven and earth. Therefore, we go and make disciples as we live under the exalted Lord. We share the glorious message of the resurrection: death and sin are defeated foes, through Jesus Christ our Lord. We shall fill up the whole earth with this good news. Christ is risen! He is risen indeed.

PRAYER

Christ is risen!
You are risen indeed!
You were born of a virgin.
Suffered and died,
buried and descended.
All for us.
All for *me*.
It did not end in death.
You were raised.
You ascended to the Father.
You sit there now
at the Father's right hand.
Knowing human weakness.
Knowing human frailty.
Knowing human temptation.
You love us all.
And you love me.
You intercede for us all.
You intercede for *me*.
Loving intercessor!
I believe this!
I believe in the resurrection.
I believe in your resurrection, Christ.
I believe.
Amen.

THE SECOND COMING AND JUDGMENT

When I was a kid, preachers were
always talking about the judgment,
and they made you feel afraid. I no
longer see it that way. I think all
people see a warm, bright light
when they die and go straight into
the presence of God. If there is a
hell, I think it's only for really evil
people, like Adolph Hitler or serial
killers. It's not for regular people
who do their best to live a good life.

—Joel

Joel holds a rather common opinion. He sees almost everyone
getting into heaven. He is not even sure there is a hell, and he
believes that if hell does exist it is reserved only for a few really
bad people who clearly deserve an awful punishment. Joel is a
semi-universalist. He believes that because God loves everyone
he punishes no one—well, almost no one.

Christians have debated for centuries on how wide or narrow the
path to heaven is. Many broaden the path so that nearly everyone
finds their way to heaven somehow. Others broaden it enough to

accommodate their relatives and friends while narrowing the route for others. Still others see the path to heaven as very narrow, found by only a few. We do not all agree on this path. Yet Christians have always agreed on this: Jesus Christ will return and judge the living and the dead.

At this point, the creed sifts tenses again. After a series of past-perfect tenses, it shifted to the present tense to describe Jesus' position in heaven. Now the creed moves to the future tense to describe Jesus' upcoming action: He shall come. Jesus came at the first advent and will come again at the second. The first time, he came to save the world. The next time, he will come to judge it. We do not like to talk about judgment. The very idea of a "judgment day" brings fear to many. The more popular view of God is one of endless forgiveness. Talking about judgment seems intolerant. Many Christians have so overdosed on God's grace that they get mighty close to rejecting this core doctrine. Yet the creed underlines what the Bible teaches: Christ will return in glory and judge the great and the small.

You and I, however, have nothing to fear. Indeed, judgment should bring joy to us, as we shall see.

FROM THERE

When Christ returns, he will come from the Father's side just as he did the first time. The Father and Son and Spirit work side by side—in the incarnation, in redemption, and in the final judgment. When Christ judges, he will do so as the agent of the Father, for together they share the role of judge. Christ is the executor of the Father's judgment.

THE SECOND COMING

Christians today prefer to talk about the second coming of Christ more than the final judgment. This has been the case since many evangelicals adopted the views of John Darby, a prominent speaker among the Plymouth Brethren who introduced the idea of *dispensationalism* in the 1800s. More recently, widely read books such as *The Late Great Planet Earth* and the Left Behind series have popularized one particular view of the end times. While the word *rapture* first appeared in print in Scofield's Bible in 1909, the apostle Paul does suggest the idea in 1 Thessalonians 4:17. According to this view, popular among evangelicals, all living Christians will be caught up into heaven at once on some future date, sometime before a *great tribulation* occurs. After this tribulation, Christ will return with the Christians and rule on earth for one thousand years in what is known as the *millennium.* According to the view, called *premillennialism,* the final judgment will then occur—after the tribulation and the millennial reign of Christ. Though this understanding of the end times is wildly popular today, it is a rather recent idea in the history of the church.

The creeds of the church say little on this topic, underlining only the Bible's core teaching that Christ's return and judgment are certain to happen. Christians differ on the schedule of events at the end, but all of us—Catholic, Orthodox, and Protestant alike—agree that Christ will return and judge. Christ will return personally, visibly, suddenly, and unexpectedly. He will appear as lightning flashes from the east to the west (Matt. 24:27). The apostle Paul described the second coming like that of an arriving royal potentate, accompanied by the blast of a trumpet. Paul said the dead Christians will rise first; then those who are alive and remain will be caught up to meet Christ in the air, and they will be with him forever. All this will happen as suddenly and unexpectedly as a thief breaking in at night (1 Thess. 4:13–18; 5:2). Jesus described himself returning to earth in clouds and with great glory, sending his angels to gather the elect from the ends of the earth (Mark 13:26). Throughout the history of the church, Christians have considered the second coming and judgment as the next great event on world's agenda.

The Apostles' Creed simply says that Christ will come again to judge. The creeds do not enter into the debate about how and when that will happen, nor do they say anything about the tribulation, rapture, or the millennium. We are left to debate the order of these events over coffee in small groups or seminary classrooms. What we are sure of is this: Christ died, Christ arose, and Christ will come again. And he is coming next as judge.

THE FINAL JUDGE

Jesus is the coming judge. The final judgment of Christ is related to a division of theology called *eschatology*—the study of the end times. But this important doctrine cannot be reduced to an item for debate. While we enjoy arguing about the various competing schedules of the end-time events, we must always remember that final judgment of Christ is not up for grabs. Jesus will return as the agent of God's judgment. Christ shares this role of judge with the Father, just as he shared the role of creation with the Father (John 1:3; Col. 1:16; Rom. 2:16). The risen Christ will do the judging.

So what kind of judge is Jesus? He is an all-knowing judge; nothing can be hidden from him. He sees beyond appearances and knows the deepest secrets of our hearts, even our intentions and covert thoughts. He is an almighty judge, able to execute judgment completely and finally. Christ is a righteous judge and he takes no bribes—neither our good works nor our passionate singing will sway his judgment. His judgments are fair and just; we can rely on pure and perfect justice.

The most impressive attribute of this judge is that he is human as well as divine. He is the God-man, Jesus Christ. He is one of us. Our judge knows humanity from the inside out. He needs no testimony from other witnesses to make his judgments complete. He himself was and is the man Christ Jesus who was resurrected

107

and ascended into heaven. At the same time, he is of the same substance as the Father—very God. The final judge at the end of time fully understands the human condition. He was incarnate as an infant, as a boy, teen, young adult, and a fully grown man. He knows our weaknesses. He was tempted at all points as we are, yet was without sin. He knows flesh and blood and human frailty and temptation. When facing this judge, a person cannot plead, "But I am only *human*." The final judge is human too, and very God at the same time. We know his judgment will be merciful, just, pure, fair, and righteous. There is no escaping this judgment. From his judgment there will be no appeal. Those who reject Christ should fear this judgment. On the other hand, we Christians look forward to it. Why? Because we believe on his name. In our case, the judge is our brother.

THOSE SUBJECT TO JUDGMENT

Christ will judge all—the living and the dead (1 Pet. 4:5). Augustine pointed out that this could be understood in two ways. It could be taken to mean the spiritually living and the spiritually dead, or it could just as easily refer to the physically living and dead. In either case, it means the same thing: "we must all appear before the judgment seat of Christ" (2 Cor. 5:10; and see Rom. 14:10). However, the judge's verdict is not undecided—as if he will make up his mind at the time judgment is executed. The verdict is already in motion, for "Whoever believes in him is not condemned, but whoever does not believe stands condemned already because he has not believed in the name of God's one and only Son" (John 3:18). Some last-days schedules predict that Christians will not have to appear before Christ for judgment, only his enemies will. Another view holds that we will all appear for judgment, though the positive verdict for Christians is secure because we have already believed in Christ and been adopted into God's family. Either way, there is nothing to fear for us. By grace through faith, we have been forgiven of our sins.

THE DAY OF JUDGMENT

The final judgment will occur at the end of time, but we don't know when that will be. The apostle Paul said, "He has set a day when he will judge the world with justice by the man he has appointed" (Acts 17:31). Paul did not know when that would happen, and neither do we. A dozen times since 1800, one religious leader or another has claimed to know the exact date of the final judgment. In every case, the date came and went. Those leaders did not know the day, and we don't either. Indeed, Jesus said that even the angels in heaven—and even he, while walking the earth—do not know the day or the hour (Mark 13:32). What we know is that we all have an appointment with God, and nobody will be late because he is coming to us.

THE DELAY

The first Christians expected the return of Christ during their lifetimes, but they were wrong. When Christ didn't appear as expected, some became doubters and gave up faith. Others reasoned that perhaps he had already come in a *spiritual* return—in the person of the Holy Spirit at Pentecost. Paul wrote to people in his day who thought Jesus had already come (see 2 Tim. 2:18). Most Christians eventually came to believe Christ had purposely delayed his coming. But why the delay? Because of God's great mercy: God is allowing more time for more people to repent (2 Pet. 3:9). God waits. Therefore, we wait too.

Christians, however, do not sit on a hill separated from this world, waiting to be taken up into heaven. As we wait, we work knowing that the night is coming. We work at completing Christ's final instruction—to make disciples of all nations. We preach the gospel so that others can believe and turn from their sins. God holds back the second coming because God loves the world and is not willing that any should perish. As we wait, we make every effort to be found spotless and blameless before him. We remember that his patience extends the opportunity for salvation to others (2 Pet. 3:14–15). We work to bring his kingdom of Christ on earth as yeast in a loaf of bread—spreading quietly and surely through the whole earth. This is a task that we will not be able to finish, but we work at it until Christ comes again and completes the history of time.

THE FEARSOME SIDE OF JUDGMENT

Christians have nothing to fear in the final judgment, but the enemies of Christ should be terrified by it. All will be held accountable. Nobody gets away with murder in the end. With the judgment comes a sorting. Christ will sort the sheep from the goats, some to the right and others to the left (Matt. 25:31–32). Some will enter into the eternal presence of God, while others will go away into darkness where there is weeping and gnashing of teeth. They will be consigned to punishment that was prepared for the Devil and his angels (Matt. 25:31, 44, 46). In the Middle Ages, lurid paintings depicting the anguish of the wicked became popular. Today we speak less of this painful side of judgment in our attempt to make Christianity more palatable to non-Christians. Nevertheless, heaven and hell are in the Bible, and while we may speak less of hell, it is nevertheless real. Certainly we are not gleeful at the torment of Christ's enemies, but we know they all will one day face our Master and hear him say, "Depart from me, I never knew you." These enemies of Christ are not all from the world. Some of Christ's enemies hide in the church, where they plunder the righteous. These may plead their case telling how they have prophesied in his name or cast out demons and even performed miracles. Christ will know that they had no real love of Christ in their hearts to back up their impressive deeds. They will be strangers to the judge (Matt. 7:22–23). However, for the folk

111

of faith, there is nothing to fear. How do we know we have nothing to fear? We know. We know our own hearts, and we know our faith. And God knows. The only individuals who should fear the judgment are Christ's enemies and strangers. If you are related to Christ, you are in.

THE JOY OF JUDGMENT

The judgment brings us Christians great joy when we understand what judgment means. Judgment is not just about punishing the guilty. Certainly, rapists who got away with rape will get what they deserve in the end. The chieftains of business who preyed on the poor while lying and stealing to enrich their own lives will pay the price. Child abusers, murderers, and adulterers who did their dirty deeds in secret will be found out. But that is only half the story. There is another side to justice. When sin's victims cry out for justice, they call for more than punishment for the perpetrator; they want things to be made right. No sentence for perpetrators can bring wholeness again to the victim of rape or sexual abuse. No penalty of our courts can bring a murder victim back to life. Our court's paltry attempts at justice pale compared to Christ's. We can punish, but we cannot make whole again. Only Christ can bring this perfect justice. When the Bible calls for justice for the poor or oppressed, it does not mean punishing the rich. It means eliminating poverty and oppression.

This is the fuller meaning of justice—making things right—and that is what brings us joy.

At Christ's final judgment, all things will be made right. This is why there is joy in judgment. We shall not live forever in a world of sin and cancer and pain and violence. We are not destined to be forever a recovering victim. This is not God's will. Judgment ushers in the kingdom of God, and this kingdom shall have no end (as the Nicene Creed states it). The kingdom of God is where his will is done on earth as it is in heaven. This is what judgment brings: all things will be restored. The world will become the way God intends it to be. All things will be brought under the auspices of Christ. All things will be made new. The sick will be fully recovered, the partial made whole, the broken healed. There will be a new heaven and a new earth. Christ will wipe away every tear. Sin will be banished forever from his kingdom. Christ will fix everything that is wrong with our world. The final "It is finished" will echo into eternity. Christ's mission to redeem all creation will be complete. This is why the judgment brings good tidings of great joy.

We humans cry for this final complete redemption every day. Every parent who has sat at the bedside of a dying child yearns for it. A woman who watches her husband waste away in the grip of cancer longs for it. The victims of shameful crime and unmentionable sin hunger for this. We know in our hearts that it must happen, or God cannot be good. And God *is* good.

In the end, all things will be made new. All wrongs will be righted. All the foes of Christ will be banished from the kingdom, and we will dwell in the house of the Lord forever.

WHAT ABOUT US

What shall we say? How shall we respond to Christ's second coming and judgment? We do not fear. We yearn for it. When we watch the news, we are tempted to despair. But we do not despair. We ache at the pain sin brings, war and famine and suffering and millions of abortions. We know there is an end. God will bring it to an end. One day all will be made right. All will be new. We know it. We cannot prove it to scoffers or unbelievers, but God has given us faith to believe it. We have bet our lives on it. Christ will come and make all things right. It is sure.

Until then, we work until the Master comes. We gather his precious harvest and bring it to his feet. We proclaim the joyful sound that Jesus saves. We rejoice that sin, death, and pain are already defeated. They will disappear forever on that day. We do not know this only because of verses here and there. We also know it because of the character of God—God is loving, just, pure, and fair, and his Son Jesus Christ our Lord died to restore the entire world. We say, "The sooner the better." The hope of that final judgment has caused Christians of all times to join John in his closing words of the book of Revelation: "Amen. Come, Lord Jesus."

PRAYER

You are coming again, Lord.
To make things right.
To end this stage of the world.
To right all wrongs.
To bring justice.
To make things new.
Because you love.
You have defeated death and sin.
Pain will be gone.
Suffering will end.
Death will vanish.
All will be new and right.

I yearn for this day, Lord.
Come to make things right.
Bring your kingdom to pass.
Thy kingdom come.
Thy will be done.
Come soon.
I believe you are coming again
to judge the living and the dead.
I'm waiting.
I'm looking forward to it.
Come soon, Lord Jesus.
I believe in your coming again.
I believe.
Amen.

I believe in the Holy Spirit.
—Apostles' Creed

THE HOLY SPIRIT

I figure what you got in the
Trinity is this: first you got
the Father, and he's the head
honcho, the Big Man. Then
you got this Son, and he's
the number two. He does
whatever the Father tells him.
Then you got the Holy Spirit,
who is like the kid brother. His
job is to do all the stuff the
other two don't want to do.
—Kurt

The Trinity is not mentioned explicitly in Scripture, though it is implicitly taught constantly. Early Christians worked out what the many biblical references to the members of the Trinity mean. The Bible speaks of God as Father and Jesus Christ as God made flesh. It also speaks of the Holy Spirit, and treats the Spirit as God also. That these three work together as one God is our belief in the Trinity. Kurt wrongly sees the Trinity as a hierarchy in which the Father sits at the top God and the Holy Spirit is some lesser kind of assistant God. Christians believe that the three persons of the

Trinity are coequal: the Spirit is very God just as the Son is God. There are three persons but one God.

The third section of the Apostles' Creed affirms that the Holy Spirit is God and not just the kid brother of the Trinity. The Holy Spirit is the link between Christ and the church—so we shall soon speak of the church. Without the Holy Spirit, the church would be just another charitable organization. With the Holy Spirit, the church is the living presence of God's kingdom on earth—the body of Christ.

THE INVISIBLE HOLY SPIRIT

We Christians believe the Holy Spirit is in our world and active. It makes us sound strange, particularly if we use the archaic name Holy Ghost, as if we were talking about some Halloween character. This is why most of us today use the title Holy Spirit. Both names emphasize the fact that the third person of the Trinity, like the Father, is not a physical but a spiritual being. We Christians actually believe that God the Holy Spirit lives, moves, and works in an invisible realm that we humans cannot see with our eyes or examine with our latest scientific instruments. Atheists and naturalists think we are off our rocker. They say this is all in our minds or that we are deluded by preachers and superstition. They claim there is no invisible world and nothing exists that cannot be seen or measured by our highly refined equipment. We Christians know better. We believe in another story of reality. We say there is a spiritual world and the Holy Spirit is real and active and works in our lives. They say, "I don't believe it." We respond, "I believe in the Holy Spirit."

DRAWING THE SHORT STRAW

We admit on first glance that the Holy Spirit seems to be snubbed in the Apostles' Creed. The Nicene Creed gives greater detail about the matter, but the Apostles' Creed says only, "I believe in the Holy Spirit." However, the Holy Spirit's apparent lack of ink is not a slight. The Holy Spirit has already been mentioned in the creed—Jesus was "conceived by the Holy Spirit." And the list of creedal affirmations that follows this second reference to the Holy Spirit delineates his work in activating the church. It is true, however, that in spite of this strong mention in the creeds, the third person of the Trinity usually draws the short straw in today's church. The Spirit is often treated as the Cinderella of the Trinity who got left home from the ball. His work is often credited to others, assigned to the Devil, or dismissed as human accomplishment. That is not true among all Christians, of course. In the early days of the Holiness Movement, people paid very close attention to the Holy Spirit and his Pentecostal power, just as charismatic churches do today.

THE DANGEROUS ONE

People get jumpy around the Holy Spirit because he has two sides. The Spirit can come like a refreshing breath of soft wind that brings encouragement and comfort. And the Holy Spirit can also come like a hurricane-force wind that is dangerous and unpredictable. At some times, the Spirit arrives as a tender dove or soothing oil, then later comes as a raging fire or whirling tornado. Since most of us prefer a polite religion that is predictable and discreet, the Holy Spirit makes us nervous. God the Father seems safe enough for some, since we can easily place him way back at the creation of the world or else way up high in the sky. And Jesus is easy enough to accept because we can think of him as a historical figure who suffered and died two thousand years ago. But the Holy Spirit is right here, right now, and is as unpredictable as the weather. That makes us edgy. When the Holy Spirit comes in our midst, things can get out of control. Most of us dislike losing control—even to the Holy Spirit.

We should admit, however, that not all extreme manifestations of spiritual power are from the Holy Spirit. Not all praising, shouting, running the aisles, speaking in tongues, healings, exorcisms, and "getting blessed" come from the Spirit. Some manifestations spring from human emotion or even carnal passion. It is easy to confuse the work of the Holy Spirit with the work of humans. We can credit the Spirit for what, in reality, are our own inner passions. This is why we place some restraints on emotional manifestations of our religion and favor the sensible, cognitive elements of our gatherings. We are not bad for doing this. Just safe. We would be delighted to "let the Holy Spirit loose" if we knew for sure it was the Spirit and not the flesh. Since it is hard to tell, we keep a lid on things. What we need today is the ability to know the difference between human activity and that of the Holy Spirit himself. We need *spiritual discernment*. However, even as we practice this discernment, we do so based on faith and not based on suspicion. We really believe that there is a Holy Spirit. We affirm as Christians that we believe in the invisible Holy Spirit who is unseen and here among us doing things. We always have believed this, and we still do.

THE HOLY SPIRIT IS GOD

The Holy Spirit is a person, not just a force. We may easily recite the words, "I believe in the Holy Spirit" today, forgetting how far people at times have departed from this orthodox truth. Some still do. One error has been to understand the Holy Spirit as a *force* or *effect* of the Father and not a distinct person of the Trinity. In an effort to avoid creating a third god, a few Christians, beginning in the early twentieth century, wandered outside historic orthodoxy into the heresy of believing that only Jesus is God. They are sometimes called "Jesus only" people. They insist that all who were baptized in the name of the Father, Son, and Holy Spirit are not truly Christian. It is a doctrinal error to reject the Trinity. The Holy Spirit is not just the invisible presence of Jesus, as some would say, and God the Father is not merely Jesus-up-in-heaven. The Holy Spirit is a third person of the Trinity. There is one God, who exists in three persons. Some Christians tend to refer to the Holy Spirit as an "it" rather than a "him." Yet the Holy Spirit is a person, not a thing. Some others fall into the error of seeing the Holy Spirit as a created being—a *creature* made by the Father, a sort of super angel—rather than God the Holy Spirit. Even if we avoid these less-than-orthodox notions, it is still easy to see the Holy Spirit as less than equal with the Father—to see him functioning as a third-in-command of the Trinity. All of these mistakes fall short of long-standing Christian belief. True Christians all agree on this: the Holy Spirit is coequal with the Father and Son, and of the same substance—that is, whatever the Father and Son are, the Holy Spirit is. The Holy Spirit was not an afterthought but existed from the beginning. When the ancient church baptized believers it affirmed this belief, saying: "I baptize you in the name of the Father, and of the Son, *and of the Holy Spirit*" (emphasis added). This is precisely how Christ commanded that we baptize. We believe in the full divinity of the Holy Spirit. The Holy Spirit is very God, just as Jesus Christ is very God, but is distinguished from the Father and the Son. Jesus told us about the Holy Spirit, and we believe he told the truth.

WORSHIP OF THE HOLY SPIRIT

At first, Christians could just say they believed in the Holy Spirit and let it go at that—as does the Apostles' Creed. However, when mistaken understandings arose, the church responded with more specific statements in the creeds. The mention of the Holy Spirit in Apostles' Creed was given more detailed comment the Nicene Creed. The church did not discover these additional phrases; they were assumed all along in the simpler phrases until someone came along preaching mistaken doctrines. The Nicene Creed specifically states that the Holy Spirit is God with the phrase "proceeds from [out of] the Father and the Son." It also states unequivocally that the Holy Spirit is the same Spirit "who spoke by the prophets." The strongest statement of all, leaving no doubt about the coequality of the Holy Spirit, is this one: "who with the Father and Son together is worshipped and glorified." Christians believe it is appropriate to sing songs of praise to Christ or to the Holy Spirit or to the Father—for in each case, we worship the same God: the Holy Trinity.

THE HOLY SPIRIT'S WORK

Perhaps the best way to wrap our practical minds around the importance of the Holy Spirit is to look at what he does. The Holy Spirit's *office,* meaning work, shows how important he is. Consider how much richer we are for his nearby presence in our lives. Reflect now on your own life and see what he has done for you. This is the Holy Spirit's work.

Drawing

The Holy Spirit drew us to himself when we were lost in darkness. Without the drawing power of the Holy Spirit, we would never have found our way. We would have never even wanted to find God. The Spirit gave us the gift of wanting to find God. The Holy Spirit got us interested and drew us toward Christ.

Convicting

The Spirit convicts the world of sin. The Spirit convicts us of our sin. Without the Spirit, we would have merrily sinned on, completely oblivious to our condition. The Holy Spirit came and convicted us of our sin and we hungered for a remedy: forgiveness and cleansing. Thank God for conviction.

Igniting Faith

The Holy Spirit sparked our faith. We think *we* decided one day to believe in Christ, but we are wrong. When we were lost in darkness we did not have the power to decide for Christ. We are soil, and soil cannot create the seed of faith. The Holy Spirit ignited the power to believe within us. Therefore, even our faith is a gift of God and cannot be claimed as a human attainment. We are a lighter with no flint. The Spirit struck the first spark of our faith so that we could believe. All we did was submit to God—we "refused to refuse" his grace.

Giving Life

The Spirit gave us new life. The Nicene Creed refers to the Holy Spirit as "the Lord the giver of Life." We have new life because he gave it to us. We were once dead in trespasses and sins, but were made alive unto God. The Holy Spirit raised us from death to life—he converted us. The Holy Spirit breathed into us the breath of eternal life. We live because the Holy Spirit brought life to us.

Indwelling

The Holy Spirit came to dwell inside us at conversion. We say that we "received Christ," but we mean that we received the Holy Spirit and were united with Christ by the Spirit's indwelling presence. If we do not have the Holy Spirit, we are not one of God's. The moment we were converted, the Holy Spirit came to live in us. We do not address God the Spirit as being out there somewhere but as in here. God the Holy Spirit indwells us.

Comforting

The Holy Spirit brings spiritual balm to comfort us. He binds us up where we are broken, soothes us where we are troubled, and

relieves us when there is pain. God the Holy Spirit is a person—
and these are the acts of a compassionate person. Are you troubled
now? You are never without hope; comforting is the Spirit's work.

Guiding

The Spirit guides us for tomorrow. He nudges us to choose
one path over another. When we trust God with all our hearts and
do not rely on our own understanding, we discover that God the
Holy Spirit directs our paths.

Teaching

The Holy Spirit is the master teacher of every Sunday school
class and the preacher-behind-the-preacher in every local church.
We may think we have been taught by a gifted teacher, proficient
pastor, or insightful author, but it is actually the Holy Spirit who
invisibly leads us into all truth. The Spirit reminds us of that truth
later. Indeed, one of the Holy Spirit's reliable works is to constantly
remind us of what we are constantly forgetting.

Cleansing

The Holy Spirit cleanses us from sin. The Spirit indwells all
Christians, but initially he cohabits with some things that do not
belong in our lives. There are words, thoughts, and deeds that
are alien to a believer's life. These habits are too strong for us
to defeat on our own. It will take the "strong man" of the Spirit

to bind them and expel them from our lives (see Matt. 12:29). Are you now free of a sinful habit you once suffered from? It was the Spirit who set you free, whether it took place gradually or in a single moment. Are you still in bondage to some sin? Cheer up, and cry out. The Holy Spirit will do more than forgive you. He can cleanse you and set you free. Seek him, for he is not far away.

Filling

The Spirit fills us as he did the disciples. Besides the ministry of subtraction in cleansing, the Holy Spirit also has a ministry of addition—filling and empowering us. We ordinary people can be filled and empowered by the Spirit so that we will be able to do what God commanded us to do: love him with all our heart, mind, soul, and strength, and love our neighbor as ourselves. We cannot do these things when we are filled with the world or with ourselves but only when filled with the Spirit. It is the Spirit's work to fill us. When we are filled with the Spirit, we will be filled with love for God and others. Ask him and see.

The Holy Spirit is more than a force or an "it." The Spirit is a person. He can be grieved or lied to. He is present and is very God just as the Son and the Father are God. He is worthy of worship and adoration. He may be dangerous, but he is good.

WHAT ABOUT US

What shall we say? Where would we be without the third person of the Trinity, the Holy Spirit? He drew us toward God, convicted us, sparked our faith, Then, when, we were converted, the Spirit gave us life and indwelled us. As we live every day, he comforts, guides, and teaches us, and offers to cleanse and fill us. This is the ordinary everyday work of God the Holy Spirit. How else can we respond to this than to adore and worship the Holy Spirit right along with the Father and the Son? Of course we shall praise the Holy Trinity—God the Father, God the Son, and God the Holy Spirit.

PRAYER

Come, Holy Spirit, we need you.
Come on your church today.
Bring us your guidance and power.
Bring us your comfort and cleansing.
Fill us all with your love.
Empower us to live like Jesus.
Come on us all today.

Come Holy Spirit, *I* need you.
Come on me now, today.
Bring me your guidance and power.
Bring me your comfort and cleansing.
Fill me up with your love.
Empower me to live like Jesus.
Come on *me* now, today.

I believe in the Holy Spirit.
I believe in you, Holy Spirit.
Do your work in my life.
I believe.
Amen.

I believe in . . . the holy catholic Church,
the communion of saints. . . .
—Apostles' Creed

THE HOLY CATHOLIC CHURCH

We're Christians, but don't
go to church anymore. We finally
got fed up with all these so-called
Christians who are really just
hypocrites. The church just isn't
relevant anymore. So we quit
being churchgoers and became
Jesus-followers. That's why we
come out here every Sunday
morning to play golf. We feel
closer to God here on the golf
course than we ever felt inside a
church with all those Christians.
—Brian and Kevin

Brian and Kevin represent a new kind of Christianity that has
become increasingly popular, especially in America. They call
themselves Christian but have divorced the church. In some ways,
it is easy to understand. With all the fallen Christian leaders and
news stories of sexual abuse by priests, it is tempting to disconnect
from the church and go it alone. This is not new, however. There
have always been people who shunned the church and tried to be
lone-ranger Christians. It does not work. This individualized
brand of Christianity passes away in just one generation. These

folk may call themselves Christians without a church, but the Bible calls them backsliders (see Heb. 10:25–27).

The church is God's gift to us. We Christians believe there is such a thing as *the* church. We believe the church is not a mere human organization like the Red Cross or the Elks Club but was created by the Holy Spirit and given to us as a means of grace for our good and our growth. It is God's creation. The world looks at the church and sees just another nonprofit organization. We look at the church and see a special creation of God's love. The church looks like a human organization, but we know it is God's creation, designed for getting people saved and baptized, for bringing his family together at the Lord's Supper, and for fostering collaboration on evangelism, discipleship, fellowship, worship, and service. To us, the church is like an extension of the incarnation. God became incarnate in Jesus Christ, and now the church is the body of Christ on earth. This is why people like Brian and Kevin, who have quit being a part of the body of Christ in order to go golfing on Sunday mornings, are in grave spiritual danger. People who say they love Jesus but despise the church attempt to behead Christ—taking the Head while rejecting the body.

ONE CHURCH

Ultimately, there is only one church. Admittedly, it takes a leap for us today to affirm the Christian church as one. The

Apostles' Creed does not use the term *one,* but the Nicene Creed speaks of "one, holy catholic and apostolic church." We Christians believe in the unity of the church—meaning all believers everywhere and at all times. Unity is not the first thing that pops into our minds when we think of the church. Yet, in spite of the fact there are hundreds of denominations and many thousands of congregations, we affirm that the church is indeed one. What do we mean when we say this? We mean that we are one against the Enemy and one in the purpose of the Great Commission. Belief in one church means there are no Wesleyans, Baptists, Presbyterians, or Roman Catholics in the real church; there are only members of Christ's kingdom. Christ is our one Head, and under him there is neither male, nor female, slave nor free, Nazarene nor Methodist.

We are one in our core beliefs too. This is why we share the creeds—we all affirm these core doctrines, as we do the Lord's Supper. We have some differences on the edges, pet doctrines like eternal security, entire sanctification, tongues, or views of the rapture, but we agree on the core matters of faith. We are one on these things. We stand shoulder to shoulder with other Christians around the world affirming, these core beliefs even if we fail to recite the creeds in our public services or have never memorized them. We believe them. When we say that the church is one, we remind ourselves that our denomination does not have a trademark on the name *Christian.* We share this name with millions of

133

others. The church is the place where the dividing walls between human beings are being overcome and a new humanity is being formed. We are one in the bond of love.

A HOLY CHURCH

While it may seem incredible to say the church is one, it is even harder to say the church is holy. It seems that we are constantly hearing yet another report of misconduct by a Christian leader or wrongdoing within the church. We see anger, jealousy, malice, bitterness, envy, and strife in the church. There is sometimes avarice, power grabbing, a judgmental spirit, adultery, and lying. The church appears to be *un*holy, not holy. How can we say we believe in one holy church?

Luke Timothy Johnson calls this sort of thing "the scandal of appearances." That is, we Christians often believe a thing against all appearances to the contrary. We believe God is Creator even though it looks as if the world may have come about naturally. We claim God heals even though all Christians eventually die, just like everybody else. We believe in a future resurrection of our bodies even though it appears that the bodies we bury disintegrate and disappear into dust. Likewise, we believe the church is holy even though it has some bad eggs in it.

When saying that the church is holy, we do not mean that it is perfect. The church is not perfect, and neither are you and I.

134

Nevertheless, the church is holy. By one holy church, we mean that the church belongs to God. The church is not of this world—it is God's and thus is holy. We believe God birthed the church and dwells with us when we gather. Holiness denotes *otherness*. The church is of heaven, of God. God has sanctified the church—set it apart for his own purposes. Our programs will die and our buildings will rot, but the church will last forever, for the church is going to heaven. The church is holy because it belongs to God.

There is more. God the Holy Spirit is at work making the church holy *in fact*, not only by virtue of that fact that God owns it. The Spirit is sanctifying the church, bringing its actual performance up to its theoretical position in Christ. Holiness is not just a labeling gimmick God uses to fool us, declaring that we are holy when in fact we are just the opposite. Holiness is also a work of the Spirit, cleansing and preparing a church to be spot- and wrinkle-free. The church is at the same time theoretically holy because it belongs to God and actually holy because the Holy Spirit is making it so. We are Christ's beloved bride, and he is cleansing us to be joined with him for all eternity.

135

A CATHOLIC CHURCH

We Protestants hesitate to say the word *catholic* in the creeds because we do not understand what the word means. To us, the term seems to refer to the Roman Catholic church, one particular denomination. Naturally, we resist making the statement that this one denomination is the one-and-only legitimate church, and rightly so. However, the word *catholic* means universal, or varied, or world-wide. The name Roman Catholic is something of an oxymoron because it uses a single location, Rome, to modify a term meaning "everywhere." The descriptive term *catholic* cannot be modified. It means that the one true church exists all over the world.

When we speak of one catholic Church, we mean that the church of Jesus Christ includes all kinds of people. The church includes different genders, races, nationalities, political parties, and worship styles, not just the kind of people in my local church. We Christians have a loyalty above class or race or nation or political party; we are citizens of another land and are just passing through this one as pilgrims. We are members of the one catholic Church that includes all kinds of people—most of them very different from ourselves.

When we speak of the one catholic Church, we are also speaking of geography. The church is catholic in that it exists around the globe. It has spread from a tiny corner of Palestine to all parts of the world. There are Christians from every nation and every tongue and tribe on the planet—we are a catholic Church, not a national church. Yet catholic means even more.

The church is universal as to time. It includes all those who have already died in the faith—those who have gone before us. The church includes James, John, Priscilla, Phoebe, and the apostle Paul. It includes Augustine, Saint Theresa, Saint Francis, John Calvin, John Wesley, Phoebe Palmer, and you and me.

The church is catholic in geography, in time, and in the variety of its members. And when we recite the creed, we confess that we are a part of this mammoth and diverse communion of saints, past and present.

AN APOSTOLIC CHURCH

The church to which we belong is *apostolic*. Some Christians get nervous about that term because it conjures the idea of *apostolic succession,* which is the notion that bishop of Rome has the authority of Christ that was given to Peter, passed on from pope to pope. Or it may make you think of some bizarre Protestant sect that permits the pastor to have exceptional power over people because he or she claims "apostolic authority." However, the creed means neither of these things.

By *apostolic,* we mean that the church we are a part of has a connection to the one established by the original apostles upon the foundation of Jesus Christ. We picture the verses in Revelation that describes the twelve foundation stones of the New Jerusalem, each bearing the inscribed name of an apostle (see Rev. 21:14). The church is apostolic because it resembles the one founded by the apostles. It continues the work of the apostles, which was given to them by Christ. That we are an apostolic church means

137

that we are engaged in carrying out the Great Commission. We are apostolic because we practice the apostolic succession of the *mission*. Jesus Christ commissioned the apostles to go, baptize, and teach people to obey Christ's teaching. We do not need to invent a new mission but to finish the old one: completing the original Great Commission given to the apostles.

THE COMMUNION OF SAINTS

The church to which we belong is a great communion of all saints. When we say we believe in the communion of saints, we are not talking about the Lord's Supper, as important as that is. This phrase is a continuation of the phrase before it. We believe in the "holy catholic Church, the communion of saints." *Communion* means community. It means gathering. We believe in Holy Spirit-created *koinonia*—a fellowship among the family of God. The church is not some imaginary, idealistic, theoretical body of individual believers who are disconnected from other believers. This sort of thinking leads Christians into privatized religion that never fails to produce bizarre results. The church we believe in is a real gathering of real people who meet in actual locations and organize themselves for carrying out the work of Christ in the real world. The church is not two people who play golf on Sunday mornings and merely claim to be Christians. The church is the physical gathering of Christ's followers.

The apostles did not create a theoretical church but a real one. Their church had real people, real problems, and a real structure. God was not incarnate as an apparition but came in a physical body. Likewise, the church is not theoretical but is a visible, gathered community, just as it was in the book of Acts where it existed in cities like Corinth, Ephesus, and Philippi. Is it true that some of the people who attend church today are not really Christians? Certainly. Yet we know this: all true believers become part of a church gathering eventually. Follow a true believer long enough, and you will find a *community* of believers that is committed to worshiping together, evangelizing the world, serving others, training believers, and sharing one another's concerns. All true Christians are a part of a church; there is no other way to be a Christian.

We are most fully the church when we gather. When Jesus announced that he would build his church, he used the Greek word *ecclesia*, which means assembly or gathering. The church of Christ always gathers. Some religions, such as Buddhism, can be practiced completely alone in the privacy of one's bedroom or garden. Not the Christian religion. Christ-following is communal. Christians are part of a family. So Christians assemble themselves together. Since the word *church* means assembly, we are *only* the church, fully and completely, when we assemble. Unassembled and dispersed, Christians can be no more than an eye or an ear. Only together do we form the body of Christ. To us, the phrase "communion of saints" especially refers personally to the visible,

139

tangible, local church congregation where we attend. The church right here, right now, this church, *my church*. My local church is a creation of God and is his gift to me.

My local church is connected to a vast communion of saints. We have communion with all Christians around the world today, plus all the saints who have already died and gone before us. We are surrounded by a great cloud of witnesses. Your godly grandmother is a part of this communion, as is the Christian you never met from Uganda. Thus, we might attend a tiny church, but that body is connected to millions of other Christians around the world, past and present. This, too, is what we mean by "the communion of saints." So there is no such thing as a small church. There are only small local gatherings of Christians that are connected to a massive communion of saints past and present. We share with this colossal communion of saints the communion of gifts, the communion of love, and the communion of resources. We can even read books by some of these saints who died fifteen hundred years ago. We are part of a huge extended family, no matter what size gathering we attend every week. This is the communion of the saints.

140

WHAT ABOUT US

What shall we say? God loved us so much that he gave to us his church who also loves us. And he gave us a church we can love. In the church we find fellowship, friendship, care, and restoration. In the church we receive solace and tenderness and meals carried in when our kids go to the hospital. In our church God gives us preaching and teaching and correction and rebuke as means of grace to make us grow. In the church we are baptized and share the Lord's Supper and pray together. In the church we find others who love Christ and want to sing praises to our God, and together we offer ourselves and our gifts to God just like the ancient Hebrews and early disciples did. In the church, we find others who want to win the lost and serve the poor and correct injustice. The church is God's gift of love to us. It is our family. Our church. This church. My church.

We will celebrate the church as a gift of God, knowing that it will endure. We know it is far from perfect. It is God's church and the gates of hell will not prevail against it. The world can criticize the church if they want. They can deride it and make fun of it, scoff at it, tax it and persecute it—but the church of Jesus Christ will endure. Nations and empires have come and gone, but the church is still here. Persecutions have risen, yet the church flourished even while they martyred our faithful. Trends have come and vanished, inventions have swept the world then disappeared, but the church prevails. The Devil fights the church daily but he cannot win. The church endures. General Motors will one day pass away. All of today's TV shows will someday seem so quaint. Our grandchildren will not even know what to do with an iPod or a cell phone, but the church will still be here. Apple computers will be antiques—indeed computers, cars, and airplanes (as we

141

know them) will one day be foggy memories, as are steamboats, stagecoaches, and papyrus today. The church of Jesus Christ will march on into eternity. Why? Because the church is the handiwork of God. It is made by God and led by the Holy Spirit. It is his church, "one holy catholic Church, the communion of saints," and the Devil cannot defeat it. The church is going to heaven and we are going with it.

PRAYER

Thank you for giving the church, Lord.
One body of Christ worldwide.
For the people who love and care for me.
I need all their care and their love.
Thanks for the body of Christ.
One body and yet many parts.
Thanks for communion and caring
and for helping me to be a good part.
Make me a more helpful member,
bringing your peace and love to the parts.
Help me to tell those not with us
about your unfailing love.
Forgive me for snubbing your body.
And help me to find my right place.
Prepare us to be your great lover,
and take us all home as your bride.
I believe in your church, dear Father.
I believe.
Amen.

THE HOLY CATHOLIC CHURCH

THE FORGIVENESS OF SINS

Oh, I don't know if I'd say that I've sinned—you know, I've always been a good girl. But I do admit I've made mistakes. And maybe sometimes I come across to other people in a way they'd consider sin, but I don't really mean it. So I wouldn't call that sin, actually. As far as God is concerned, I'm pretty sure he wouldn't hold those things against me. I think he knows the situation and understands why I did some things. So I guess I can't say for sure that I've never done a real sin.

—Kaila

Kaila is a product of today's culture. She admits she has done wrong things, but she doesn't consider her wrongdoing "sin." She sees God as the Great Understander—dismissing her sins as minor misunderstandings. Kaila cannot be forgiven, for she confesses no sin. When we say we believe in the forgiveness of sin, we do not just mean other people's sins—we mean our own.

Christians believe in sin and the forgiveness of sins. The creed now is about to wind up. We will soon look forward to a glorious future: the resurrection of the body and life everlasting.

This is our glorious destiny. Yet we enter this future only through the doorway of the forgiveness of sins. We confess that we believe our sins can indeed be forgiven leading to this future. This section of the creed falls into the work of the Holy Spirit and the church to whom God has provided the "keys" to the kingdom and forgiveness.

WE BELIEVE IN SIN

We need to start by stating there is such a thing as sin before we go on to speak of forgiveness. Indeed, Christians believe in such a thing as sin. Today it is harder to get people to believe in sin than in forgiveness. They might admit they are sinners, but when asked to specify they really cannot list a single thing, like Kaila at the beginning of this chapter. Can there be forgiveness if there is no sin? Of what would we be forgiven—bad taste?

We don't like to talk about sin. This is not new. It has been true since Adam and Eve. When we do evil, we tend to blame others. We offer excuses and mitigating circumstances. "But, I didn't mean it," we plead. We explain, "I had too much to drink," or "My father abused me," so we can pin the responsibility on some other person or thing. We admit "my mistake," then sign up for counseling or sign into recovery. These things are helpful, but if we use them to duck responsibility for sin, they hurt us more than help.

Christians believe there is such a thing as sin. We believe there are transgressions because there are laws. Sin is trespassing, a deviation from God's will. Christians say, "Sin exists" to a world that disbelieves us. We believe this moral law is established by God and not set by government, votes, or courts. Something may be legal or even admired in a culture, but we believe it is sin if God says so. In a world that decides the standard of sin by elections or tells us we can decide for ourselves, Christians counter that the law of God is external and not up for amendment.

Sin, however, is more than an act; it is also a *state* of rebellion against God. Sin is something internal, something wrong with humanity. When we say there is forgiveness from sin, we are speaking of a remedy for both sinning acts and the state of sinning. People sin and sinners are guilty. By "guilty" we do not mean they *feel* guilty; a great number of sinners do not feel the slightest twinge of guilt. We mean they *are* guilty. To us guilt is not a feeling but a fact. Breaking God's laws or even refusing to believe in God brings objective guilt. The sinner might feel as carefree as a canary, but he or she is *in fact* guilty. We have all sinned and we are all responsible. Like sheep, we have all gone astray—all of us have sinned and fallen short of God's ideal and are in need of forgiveness. We believe in sin because we have sinned—all of us. We believe in forgiveness and cleansing from that sin.

147

WE BELIEVE IN FORGIVENESS

We call the gospel "good news," and now we see why; to be delivered from sin is good news. All of us have broken God's laws and deserve punishment, yet forgiveness came to us. We were sinners by state and rebellious against God, but we were changed. We could not get relief from our guilt by forgiving ourselves or even getting forgiveness from others. We did not make the laws; God did. All sin is against God first: "Against you, you only, have I sinned" (Ps. 51:4). Only the Lawgiver could grant us forgiveness. Forgiveness was outside us. There was nothing we could do to make up for our sin. We could not pay off our debt. Forgiveness came free to us and we accepted it. In our creeds, we confess our belief in this story. We transgressed and were guilty. God forgave us. Our sins were buried in the depths of the sea—removed as far as the east is from the west. Our sins are gone.

We Christians are not individuals who lived better than others and thus got inducted into the church. We did not get in because we were the nicer half of society. We were ordinary sinners and rebels against God, but God forgave us, saved us, and made us into his children; and he has provided forgiveness and cleansing from sin. Some of us were prostitutes and thieves, murderers and adulterers. Others of us told white lies, gossiped, and were self-absorbed. Yet God forgave us all. The notion seems too impossible to believe. It seems to violate our sense of justice.

How could God forgive murderers or Christ-killers? How dare God wipe away the sins of an evil serial killer? He forgives them the same way he forgives gossips and selfish folk like me. We imagine God did not take much effort to forgive us—after all, our own sins seem so *minor*. God forgives sins great and small. He forgave you and me. God comes to the table bringing forgiveness, and I come to the table bringing . . . well, I bring nothing at all. We believe in the forgiveness of sins.

However, sin is more than breaking God's laws. At the core, sin is a broken relationship—grieving the heart of a loving God. Forgiveness is about reconciliation, not merely wiping out a debt. Forgiveness restores our broken relationship with God and others. Forgiveness brings new life to marriages, to churches, to cities, even to nations. We Christians believe in the forgiveness of sins— our own and those of others.

THROUGH CHRIST OUR LORD

On the basis of Jesus Christ's atonement God forgave us. We could not pay our debt, balance our evil, or make deposits of good works on the scales to tip the balances. Because of God's Son Jesus Christ, our sins are forgiven. Jesus is the Lamb of God who takes away the sins of the world. Christ is the atonement for sins. God himself offered himself up for our sins. Your sins. My sins. Everyone's sins. This is what we mean when we say we believe in the forgiveness of sins. Jesus paid it all. Jesus never sinned or needed forgiveness, yet he bore our sins and became the perfect sacrifice for us—and for the sins of the whole world. What wondrous love.

HOW GOD FORGIVES SINS

In Repentance and Faith

We were forgiven after our repentance and faith. We Christians reject the idea that God would decide to forgive based on our goodness, as if only the best people are forgiven. This would be earning forgiveness. Nor do many of us think God put everybody's name in a box, then drew out winners in some celestial lottery. That would be capricious, we think. And we reject the notion that God will simply forgive everybody's sins in the end, as if sin really didn't matter. So who is forgiven? We believe what the Bible says: those who *repent and believe* are forgiven.

Some might wonder if that doesn't bring us back to the notion that we're forgiven based on our own good works. When I repent and have faith, have I somehow earned my forgiveness? Not at all. It is not up to me to initiate this process; God always makes the first move. God is constantly reaching out to all men and women everywhere, drawing them toward repentance. God is active, not passive. He is reaching and drawing humanity toward forgiveness. If no missionary ever goes to a people group living

150

in some remote part of the earth—God the Holy Spirit is already there, convicting and drawing individuals toward himself. Our repentance and faith is a response to God's first steps toward us. The Holy Spirit is the master evangelist, drawing, convicting, nudging, and planting seeds.

So if the Spirit is drawing all men and women to him, why aren't they all saved? It is because some resist. When God says yes, they say no. Or they say, "Not yet" or "Later." The only action needed to be saved is to surrender to God's grace—saying yes to God's yes. We who have been forgiven have submitted to God's seed and let it grow. We refused to refuse. We could not work up faith on our own, but we submitted ourselves to his grace. As we surrendered, he saved us, forgave us, and made us his own.

In Baptism

In the ancient church, forgiveness and baptism were closely tied. This is why the Nicene Creed states, "We believe in one baptism for the remission of sins." The apostles often commanded people to repent and be baptized for the forgiveness of sins (see Acts 2:38; 3:19; 22:16). Thus, baptism quickly became wedded to forgiveness. It made sense. The symbolism of washing was a natural metaphor for the washing away of the guilt of sin. The very first Christians, who were Jews, went straight from repentance to baptism—as if they were the same thing.

Once the church's outreach moved from Jews to Gentiles, baptism was more often delayed. The Gentiles had more sinful baggage to get rid of. Gentiles often clung to other gods and carried on an immoral lifestyle emulating street dogs, as their Jewish neighbors put it. Gentiles took some time to be cleaned up before being baptized, often about two years.

Soon a new twist arose—delaying baptism until near death. Early Christians believed that baptism was the moment when God washed away all past sins. But what about future sins? They mistakenly believed that there was no remedy for sins committed after baptism. There was no second repentance or re-baptism. If a Christian chose purposeful sin after being baptized, it was curtains. (However, we should remind ourselves that these early Christians were not as introspective as modern people are. When they spoke of sin, they meant what we might call capital sins or crimes.) Thus, if a Christian was baptized but later committed adultery or offered incense to Caesar, there was no way back. A careful reader of the New Testament book of Hebrews can see this hard-line approach. Given this understanding, we can readily see why the Christian emperor Constantine waited until just before death to receive baptism. He wanted to make sure all his sins were forgiven at baptism.

Within a few hundred years, the church had come up with other remedies for any sin committed after baptism: *penance* for mortal sins, and *confession* for venial sins. Since then, only rarely have churches returned to the old hard-line position of the ancient church. This helps us see why baptism was at first closely associated with forgiveness of sins. Some denominations still believe in *baptismal regeneration,* the idea that sins are forgiven by the act of baptism, and they consider baptism the actual moment of conversion. However, most Christians recognize that he moment of new birth comes before baptism.

The Altar Call

The *altar call,* frequently used by evangelicals, fits in here, though it may seem odd to speak of a tradition that has only about a two-hundred-year history in a book dealing with the Apostles' Creed. Yet if we asked evangelical people to name the time when they received forgiveness of sins, many would say, "That happened when I received Christ." They might tell of praying in their small group or perhaps going forward at one of the mass altar calls that evangelists made famous in the nineteenth and twentieth centuries. Many in the revivalist tradition have named the altar call, or "decision to receive Christ," as the moment where forgiveness of sins is received. Revivalists still practice baptism as "an outward sign of an inward work." For revivalists, however, the actual moment of forgiveness came when they "prayed the prayer" after a presentation of the gospel message. Baptism is the public testimony to that earlier, more important, moment.

153

Revivalists have separated repentance and baptism just like the early church did when it took up the Gentile mission. Either way, we all agree that the "one baptism" is the baptism commanded in the Great Commission—baptism in the name of God the Father and of the Son and of the Holy Spirit. No other washing, baptism, or ritual will do. Whether we received forgiveness at a gas station, in a small group, or in response to an invitation, we Christians move on to finish the process of obedience by receiving baptism. While the altar call rite (or, more generally speaking, the moment of decision to receive Christ) is not practiced by all Christians everywhere, it has been a widely recognized entry rite preceding baptism for several hundred years. We all agree that recently invented rites like the altar call should not cause us to dismiss Christ-established sacraments like baptism, for that is precisely where the altar call should lead.

In the Church

Forgiveness happens in the church—the communion of saints. God has built a place where forgiveness flows—his church, the body of Christ. Those of us who call ourselves Protestants do not think much of God's idea. We would rather deal direct. The idea of going to the church to get in the flow of forgiveness irritates us. We would prefer to get our forgiveness in our garden, on the golf course, or in our private devotions. We prefer to have a personal

God, not a God who reveals himself best to a group of people—two or more gathered together—called the church.

Yet God has given the keys of forgiveness to his church, and he gave the church the right to "bind and loose" (Matt. 16:19). It astonishes many Christians to hear Christ tell the church that what it binds on earth will be bound in heaven (and what we loose here will be loosed there). We Protestants run out of the room with our hands over our ears when we hear that scripture. We are so strongly conditioned to value the sovereignty of God that we actually resent his choice to delegate this kind of authority to mere human beings. We can trust God to forgive, but we don't trust other people to hold that same power. Yet we cannot dodge the plain teaching of Christ. He handed off the keys of his Kingdom to the church. So what does this mean? How do we find forgiveness in the church?

God offers forgiveness in the church though the means of grace. And he offers forgiveness though the ordinary activities practiced by Christ's church. When a church does what the church is supposed to do, forgiveness is offered. We find forgiveness in the church through these ordinary channels of grace.

What are these ordinary channels of grace where forgiveness flows? First, we hear forgiveness offered through gospel *preaching*. How shall they believe unless they hear through a preacher? Paul asks (Rom. 10:10). In the church, we join in *confession*. Some churches actually recite a confession together each week;

others follow along as the pastor leads in confession during the pastoral prayer. Confession leads to forgiveness. Some churches regularly pray the *Lord's Prayer*, in which we ask God to forgive our trespasses each time we pray it. In the church, we receive *baptism* and hear *altar calls*—both channels of forgiveness. We do not baptize ourselves in our own bathtubs—it is the church's business, and it is a corporate act, not a private one. In the church, we get to take the *Lord's Supper*, where we are instructed to pause for a time of self-examination and confession, clearing our hearts of any sin. In the church, we attend classes, Sunday school, and small groups where the *Word of God* is taught, explained, and applied. God has promised that his Word will have a cleansing effect on us, washing away sinful habits, thought patterns, and behaviors. In the church, we especially experience *koinonia*—an accepting loving Christian fellowship that grants us lateral human forgiveness. Sometimes we only feel forgiven by God when we feel forgiven by others, which is why we were told to confess our sins one to another (see James 5:16).

The keys to the Kingdom are the ordinary activities of the church. They are our commissioned activities. The keys lead to the forgiveness, reconciliation, and restoration we find in the church. God has entrusted to us these keys—the means of grace. We control what we preach or how often we serve Communion or give an altar call. We hold the keys.

We can use these keys to open forgiveness to others, or we can lock up the Kingdom to others by treating these means of grace casually or offering them sporadically, choosing instead merely to entertain the masses. God wants us to use these keys to open the Kingdom and let forgiveness flow abundantly. When the church practices the ordinary activities of an ordinary church—preaching, Bible study, prayer, fellowship—God's forgiveness flows to the penitent. This is good news.

WHAT ABOUT US

What shall we say? Can this thing be? You and I have sinned in word, thought, and deed. In addition, our sinfulness is a broken relationship, with God and others. If our entire life's thoughts, words, and deeds were broadcast on television, we would be ashamed. Thankfully, that will not happen. The hard-drive that recorded our sins has been reformatted. The files are gone, to be remembered against us no more. We are forgiven. All charges have been dropped. We are free to go. This is not a freedom to go out but to come in. We are free to come into the home of the Judge, where we now live as his children. We want to pinch ourselves to see if it is true. Judgment is surely coming, but we know that we are not guilty.

So how do we live in the meantime? Simple: we who are forgiven become forgivers. We forgive those who sin against us just like God forgave us. We forgive freely, willingly, completely, and with no hitches. There is no such thing as partial forgiveness; forgiveness is

157

done in whole. God forgave us completely, so we forgive others likewise. We owed God millions. Others owe us a nickel, or maybe a dollar. We Christians forgive others because we have been so generously forgiven by God. This is one reason we love God so much—those who are forgiven much, love much (see Luke 7:47).

We Christians are not a vengeful people. We forgive. Go ahead and force us to carry your packages a mile. We will take them a second mile. Slap us on the face, and we will not slap you back; we will turn the other cheek. We are hard to figure out. We do not operate by the rules down here but by another set of rules from another land. This is why we do not know the word *enemy*. We cannot have enemies, because we forgive them all. You may declare yourself our enemy, but it will mean nothing to us, for we already forgave you and we now pray for you. We will forgive you even if you do not ask and do not want our forgiveness. This is just what we do.

Therefore, you enemies of Christ, go ahead, attack us and see. We will forgive you. Criticize us in the newspapers and make fun of us on television, and we will forgive you. Toss us in prison, and we will forgive you as we enter our dark cell. Stake out our husbands in the sun to die, and we will pray for you and forgive you even before they die. Whip our backs until they are bloody, place a crown of thorns on our head, and hang us on a cross, and we will say, "Father, forgive them." This is how Christians act. We forgive because we have been forgiven. We forgive those who trespass against us because we have been forgiven our trespasses against God. This is why Christians are such great forgivers. God's forgiveness of our own sins makes it easy for us to forgive those who trespass against us. This is what we mean when we say in our Creed that we believe in the forgiveness of sins.

PRAYER

What wondrous love!
That you should love the unlovely.
While we were still in trespasses and sins.
When *I* was sill sinning and hopeless.
You reached down to forgive me.
I'm forgiven and free.
Because of your unfailing grace.
I am washed by the blood of your Son.
My forgiveness is complete.
Your grace is greater than I can imagine.
Your mercy too big to comprehend.
You give me power to overcome.
To live like you taught us to live.
What wondrous grace you have given us.
Given to *me*.
Forgiveness of sins.
I believe I'm forgiven of my sins.
I believe.
Amen.

THE RESURRECTION OF THE BODY

I guess I've always believed
that when you die, they put
your body into the ground
and your atoms go back into
the earth—from ashes to ashes,
dust to dust. That's the end of
it for the cells that make up
your body—they become dirt.
But your soul goes to heaven
to be with God.

—Cassie

The phrase "resurrection of the body" perhaps inspires more unbelief among today's church attendees than any other statement in the creed. Though Christians have always taught that our physical bodies will someday be resurrected, many people today, choose to believe only in a spiritual resurrection whereby the soul goes to heaven, leaving the body behind forever. This idea of a soul resurrection is not new. Early heresies taught that the body was evil and only spirit was good; thus, heaven was a place where only spirits would dwell. Christians resisted this body-less resurrection by standing firm with the apostle Paul in insisting that our bodies, too, will be raised and will go with us into the afterlife. This is why Christians have always stated that they believe in the resurrection of the body.

Ben Franklin purportedly said that nothing is certain in this life but death and taxes. While taxes may not be certain, death definitely is. Even Jesus Christ faced death. All of us will face death unless the second coming of Christ occurs first. Death is the original question confronting humankind, and all religions attempt to answer it. Some propose that death leads to an endless round of human recycling into reincarnated beings. Other religions offer the final escape of the soul from the body into an eternal, spiritual world. The secular answer to the question of death is the flimsy hope that dead people somehow live on the memory of others. The Christian answer to death is the resurrection of the body. We believe there will be an actual, physical event in which our bodies will be raised and we, as whole persons— soul and body—will enter God's presence for eternity.

HARD TO BELIEVE

We must admit that the resurrection of the body is the least-believed claim of the Apostles' Creed. Even some Christians attempt to dodge it. A person can boldly state sub-Christian beliefs about the after life in a Sunday school class or small group and not be challenged. Even many who accept the idea of a bodily resurrection find the belief difficult to defend. We should admit that it is a preposterous belief. It is inconceivable. Christianity makes some astounding claims, such as the virgin birth of Jesus, and this belief in a bodily resurrection is one of them. By all that we know, that cannot happen. Yet Christians believe precisely that our bodies will be raised to life again. To those trained in the hard sciences, this belief sounds crazy. Yet we Christians have believed this for thousands of years, and still do.

The modern age caused some Christians to think of the resurrection as far-fetched. Some tossed it away as an unscientific myth. These folk honored only the moral teachings of Jesus. This is where the original WWJD (What would Jesus do?) movement developed. These people believed that preposterous claims of miracles or of the resurrection would push the modern world away from Christ. Therefore, they tossed these miracles overboard and packaged the moral teachings of Jesus as "a better way to live." This is how modern liberalism was born. However, these folk went down a sidetrack—a path to nowhere. Other Christians continued to believe the claims of the creed, including this one: sometime in the future, our bodies, having been buried in the ground, will rise again; and we, as physical human beings, shall live forever with Christ. This orthodox doctrine is the main track of Christianity. It is the track that always survives the sporadic waves of unbelief—even unbelief in the church.

163

It is always easier to accept this doctrine of the resurrection as applied to Jesus than to ourselves. We can accept heaven and the continued life of the soul, but the resurrection of the body? That is harder to swallow. We raise all sorts of practical objections to this belief, as if it were up to us to understand how such things work. We ask, "If I am destroyed in a fire and my cells go up in smoke, how are the cells of my body going to be recovered and put back together?" Or, "What if someone was eaten by a bear and their cells become absorbed into the cells of the bear. How are they raised—as a partial bear?" Or, "Since the body is constantly being renewed, which cells and atoms will get raised again—the ones in my body at death or a sampling of cells from my entire lifetime? How many cells does God need to recreate my body from scratch?" Our scientific minds make us want to dismiss the whole notion and lower ourselves to accept the sub-Christian view that only the soul will live forever.

Ironically, some advances in scientific knowledge have actually made this incredible doctrine easier to fathom. Scientists can now clone a duplicate body from a single cell of the donor body. The notion of recreating a body from a single cell no longer sounds preposterous, even by purely human reasoning. And just imagine how much more God can accomplish than can a human scientist.

Of course, Christians would believe this doctrine regardless of any scientific developments that make it appear more reasonable. We believe in the resurrection of the body because the Bible says it is so. It tells us that the body of Jesus has already been raised. Christ is the resurrection and the life. He is the firstfruits of the resurrection. Jesus already was raised from the dead, and the Bible tells us we will follow. We do not believe that only the soul of Jesus appeared to the disciples after his resurrection. It was not a ghost of Jesus that wandered about visiting his followers. It was the actual body of Jesus that came back to life. And was not raised, like Lazarus, only to die again. Jesus' body was raised anew and incorruptible—it would never die again. His body was different in some ways, yet it was the actual body that was buried three days before. He did not receive a rental body but received his own body back again. It seems impossible to understand, and it is hard to believe. Indeed, this doctrine must be *believed*—there is no proving it to an unbeliever. Only believers believe these things. We do so because the Holy Spirit prompts us to believe them. Therefore, even when our belief in the resurrection wavers, the Spirit reminds us in the creed of the central Christian claim: Jesus is risen, and one day we too will rise. We believe in the resurrection of the body.

165

IN THE MEANTIME

What happens to us when we die? The ancient Stoics taught that after death the physical body is simply reabsorbed into the earth and continues a cycle of use, disposal, and renewal; to them only the soul mattered. The early church also faced the Gnostic heretics, who despised the body and identified it with sin and only the soul with good. The Gnostics saw no need of the *body* being resurrected—why resurrect sinful flesh? They opted for the future state of humans to be purely spiritual—a realm of body-less souls. Christians fought back ferociously against the Gnostic heresy, arguing for the salvation and resurrection of the whole human being—body and soul alike.

Many Christians believe that people who die go to heaven immediately and are with the Lord right now floating around on clouds. That view does not require a bodily resurrection. Anyone attending a funeral can see how attractive it is to be able to say, "Your loved one is up there right now, walking the streets of heaven." There are orthodox ways of coming to this conclusion. We could say that the spirit goes to be with Christ in a temporary Spirit-heaven, and later on Christ will return with these spirits to reunite us with their resurrected bodies. We might conjecture that God supplies our spirits with a temporary body in which to dwell while we await the final resurrection, at which time we will return to our own bodies. Others imagine a kind of soul sleep which would make the many years between our death and resurrection seem to be only a moment, like taking a short nap.

Whatever we envision as the intermediate state between death and final resurrection, a Christian doctrine always ends with a real resurrection of a real body. A body-less heaven is a sub-Christian idea. While Christians may dwell in one or another state between the moment of our death and our final resurrection, the creed reminds us that we will all one day receive our bodies back. This is what we mean by believing in "the resurrection of the body."

RESURRECTION OF THE BODY

The idea of a bodily resurrection was a shared belief between Christianity and most elements of ancient Judaism. Though one Jewish party, the Sadducees, rejected the idea, most other Jewish teachers affirmed the resurrection of the body. Some early Christians may have resisted the doctrine too. Paul taught directly on this subject, perhaps because some in Corinth doubted the doctrine. While flesh and blood cannot inherit the kingdom of God, the apostle Paul taught that our actual flesh could be resurrected anew. Paul claimed "this" corruptible must put on incorruption. By that he meant the very body that he occupied as he wrote (see 1 Cor. 15:53). The resurrected body would become incorruptible, never wearing out.

Christianity can be quite material. It teaches us that these very physical bodies will someday be changed and will continue to exist. Our future is not to spiritually float around among the clouds as disembodied souls strumming spiritual harps. Christ has gone to prepare for us a *place.* We look toward a new heaven and a new earth, not spiritual worlds, but real places where we will be real people in real bodies. Some even believe we will occupy a new earth right here—an earth that is restored to the will of God. We will be changed, but we will be similar to what we are now. Redemption is not just about saving our souls, it is about redeeming and saving bodies, for we are whole persons. Indeed, redemption is about redeeming all of creation (see Rom. 8). God plans to redeem us completely, including our bodies. It is the same with salvation. God is not just interested in sanctifying our souls. He wants to sanctify us through and through, so that our "whole spirit, soul and body [will] be kept blameless at his coming" (1 Thess. 5:23). In Christian doctrine, the body is not a bad thing we are trying to escape. Christians believe in the resurrection of the body.

EVERYONE RESURRECTED

Heavily influenced by popular books and movies about the end-times, Christians today often skip the idea of the resurrection altogether and focus instead on the rapture. The rapture does make for a more dramatic story line, but the creed does not even mention the rapture. More surprisingly, both the creed and the Bible say that *all* people will be resurrected, not just Christians. Every person who ever lived—good or bad—will be raised to life again. Your great-grandmother will rise, and so will Joseph Stalin. The resurrection is not a special opportunity for Christians only—it is for all people. Perhaps that's why so many Christians prefer to talk only about the rapture: it seems to give Christians center stage.

OUR RESURRECTED BODIES

Most of us wonder what sort of body we might have in the future. Medieval thinkers thought we would all be about thirty years old, even babies, but that was mere conjecture. Who knows? When the Corinthian resurrection-doubters wanted to dwell on these kinds of questions, Paul simply called them fools (see 1 Cor. 15:35–36). We do not know exactly what our bodies will look like. We do know that the Bible promises us that one day we will have our resurrected body back and that we will live forever. Thus, we refuse to believe the lie saying our bodies are just temporary houses for our souls that will be discarded when we are through with them.

We also know that in the resurrection, we will be fully human. To be human is to be physical. To have no body is to be less than fully human. Christ did not die to help us escape humanity but to enable us to become fully and perfectly human. In the resurrection, we will find that full humanity—becoming in the flesh all that God meant us to be. Our best clues concerning our resurrected state are found in the resurrected body of Jesus. Christ's resurrected body could be seen and touched, and he could and did eat food. Yet his resurrected body was not bound by the physical laws of the universe; he could appear and disappear in a moment. It was somehow different than but related to his previous body. It appeared human to others, was recognizable by others (though not at first). These clues tell us that our future is quite physical. The doctrine of the resurrection is the ultimate affirmation of the goodness of the body and the goodness of the material world. Our final life will not be lived as floating spirits but will be a physical life in a physical body that has been resurrected from this world.

RESURRECTION FOR JUDGMENT

We are resurrected for judgment. Both the Creed and the Scriptures say the Lord will come again to "judge the living and the dead" (2 Tim. 4:1; 1 Pet. 4:5). In this case, the dead are judged after they are resurrected. The resurrection is wonderful news to Christians, for whom it signals entry into eternal bliss. But it is bad news for the enemies of God; it signals their impending judgment.

All people will get their bodies back—believers and unbelievers alike. That doesn't sound fair, does it? Why should the enemies of Christ get to come back to life too? Would it be a better system to have the Christians resurrected while unbelievers are left moldering in their graves forever? That might sound fair to us, but not to God. The Bible teaches that every human being will rise again in order to be judged. Judgment implies making a distinction or separation—the sheep will be distinguished from the goats. The former

170

will gain eternal life, the latter eternal punishment. The resurrection of the body is a double-edged sword. It should be a terrifying notion to the enemies of Christ; they should hope the Bible is wrong about this. To us who believe it is a wonderfully blessed thought. We will receive our bodies back, and they will be incorruptible. There will be no sore backs, no limping legs, no headaches. We will be able to run and not be weary, to walk and never become exhausted. Our resurrected bodies will not wear out. We will inhabit these new bodies in heaven, where we will live in everlasting love with each other and God. This is cause for celebration.

WHAT ABOUT US

What shall we say? How will we live in light of the resurrection of the body? For starters, we look forward to it, as the Nicene Creed says. We anticipate our Lord's coming and the final resurrection, even his judgment, for we have no fear of either. Our belief in the resurrection of the body makes us live like there is more to life than what we see. We Christians are not under the tyranny of materialism because we know this is not the only life there is. We treat our bodies differently because we know God respects them and intends to raise them up again. Our flesh is not bad, and our bodies are worth treating with dignity and care.

We believe in the resurrection of the body and so we believe death is not the end of life. Others are terrified by death. We are not. Death is a shadow we do not fear. At our Christian funerals, you see the effect of our belief in the resurrection. We, too, pass through the valley of the shadow of death and cry at funerals. In spite of our grief, however, there is always a note of joy. A Christian funeral is not the end of a life but a passage to another life. We Christians treat life on earth as if we are in the womb awaiting our birth. We act as if we are pilgrims here, pilgrims waiting return to our homeland.

This way of thinking is one reason so many of us have been willing to face martyrdom. Because we believe death is but a transition, we are not afraid to die. Go ahead, threaten to kill us and watch how we act. Sure, we may cry out in agony as flames lick our flesh, but Christians always die in hope. We know death cannot kill us. All you can do is destroy our bodies, and you can only destroy our bodies for awhile. We believe even our bodies will rise again to live in the presence of God forever. If you do not believe in the resurrection, you will think the martyrs are insane. But there *is* a resurrection, and we believe it. The martyrs lived as if this is true up to their last breath. You can kill a Christian, but you cannot destroy a Christian. For you cannot kill our souls, and you can kill our bodies only temporarily. We will rise again.

It is true that the grim reaper visits us just as often as he visits atheists and agnostics. Sure, we experience pain from cancer just like someone who has rejected God. However, when death comes for us, watch us very closely and see how we die. To

Christians, death is a boogeyman. It is a shadow with no teeth. It is scary, but it cannot harm. This is because we believe in the resurrection. So watch us face death and listen to what we say. Hear us say, "Oh death where is your sting? O grave, where is your victory?" We will answer for death and the grave—the sting and victory are gone through Jesus Christ our Lord. Death has been defeated. Christ defeated it for us. Up from the grave he arose. We, too, will rise as he did. Death cannot defeat us because death is swallowed up in victory. Praise the blessed name of Jesus Christ our Lord and God the Father, who raised him from the dead and who will raise us too. We believe in the resurrection of the body.

173

PRAYER

Thank you, God, for the resurrection.

I believe this body will rise.

My body is not destined for the trash heap.

You will raise it to new life.

You did it already with Jesus.

You'll do it again for me.

You will take us all to heaven.

I believe in Christ's resurrection.

But I also believe in my *own* resurrection.

I trust in your power and might.

I expect a reunion of my soul and my body.

I believe in the resurrection of the body.

I believe.

Amen.

THE LIFE EVERLASTING

I don't think too much about
heaven. I believe in it, I guess, but I
don't really talk about it or sing
songs about it like my parents did.
I'm not one of those pie-in-the-sky
types. The idea of floating around
on clouds with harps and what not
just doesn't appeal to me. When I
think of heaven, I think of a quiet
trout stream where I can be alone
every day—and where I get a hit
on every cast. That's my heaven.
—Kenny

Kenny doesn't think much about heaven, and neither do most
people. We'd rather do all we can to create heaven on earth. The
idea of escaping this world into a future world of bliss seems to
be a waste of time to folk who have it really good right now. The
better off we are here on earth, the less we speak of heaven. And
most of us, at least in America, have it pretty good right here and
now. When we do bother to imagine heaven, we tend to envision
a place that meets our expectations for earthly bliss—our version of
the perfect fishing trip. While we don't know all that much about

the afterlife, we Christians have always claimed at least this—life on earth is not all there is. We believe in the life everlasting.

DISDAIN FOR HEAVEN

Why is it that many Christians today have such contempt for otherworldliness? We say, "Even if there were no heaven, I'd live as a Christian anyway," arguing that the afterlife is irrelevant to our faith choices. We don't usually think of heaven as an actual place where Christ has gone to prepare for our arrival. We more often think of heaven as a kind of spirit world that runs parallel to us right here and now. We are pragmatic people, and heaven seems useless—especially if it consists of floating around on clouds and playing harps. However, the biggest reason we (at least in the developed world) think little of heaven may be the high quality of our lives now. Our lives are quite good, and it is no secret that the better off Christians become the less they preach or sing about heaven. If you have a good life now, you don't tend to hope for a better one. Besides, the idea of being swept up to heaven sounds a little goofy—like an alien abduction. And we don't want to be thought of as weird.

Yet there are times when we do think about the life that is to come. When we retire to a quiet eddy from our hurried lives, our thoughts turn toward heaven. The woman who puts her husband of forty years into the ground thinks about heaven. When a physician announces, "Your mother has three months to live," we quickly become pensive and ponder the afterlife. And when we ourselves discover that our time on earth is coming to an end, think very seriously about this doctrine that Christians have always believed: the life everlasting.

Here is where the Christian worldview radically departs from the secular, naturalistic explanation of life. Naturalists believe you are born, you live, you die, and that's that. Christians believe that death is not the end but the beginning. We believe we will enter eternal life. We expect to be among that number "when the saints go marching in." We cannot prove there is a heaven, but we believe it.

LIFE IN HEAVEN

John Calvin once quipped that people were far more interested in what heaven is like than in how to get there. Even today many people seem to want "fire insurance" to escape from hell but think little about what the afterlife may actually be like. So what is heaven like? We do not know as much about it as we would like. We know that Christ promised to prepare a place for us there. Our bodies will be raised, and we will go there to be with God forever. Because our bodies are going there, we know it is a physical place. We know God will be there, as will all of God's people from all times. Beyond these basics, we are left to conjecture. Heaven has been pictured as a promised land to which we are journeying—a homeland promised

177

by God. It has also been viewed as a paradise, a re-creation of the perfect Eden. We know it is like a great feast or banquet with all the celebration and intimacy that goes with it. However, we do not even know if heaven is up, or out, or right here on earth, or in some parallel universe. It is a place to be sure, but we cannot pinpoint its location. We do know that heaven is everlasting, that we shall be there in the presence of God, and that it is a *good* place.

Knowing Others

Most of us cannot imagine a heaven where we could not recognize friends and loved ones. Perhaps the most widely rejected saying of Jesus is his reply to the Sadducees in which he stated that we will neither marry nor will be given in marriage in the resurrection (see Matt. 22:30). Most Christians expect to be reunited with their parents and their spouse in heaven, no matter what Jesus said. Maybe this is okay. Jesus was making a retort to a trick question posed by some of his enemies. The question came from Sadducees, who scoffed at the idea of a resurrection. To prove that the resurrection is a ridiculous idea, they asked about a man who had had seven wives on earth. In the resurrection, they wondered, which one of them would he be married to? Jesus' answer probably should not be considered the core teaching on heaven in the Bible. We could take Jesus' words to mean that there is no awareness of ourselves as individuals in heaven, but very few people accept that idea.

There are other strains in the Bible, though, that suggest we will recognize others. In the resurrection we will come from the east and west to sit down with Abraham, Isaac, and Jacob (see Matt. 8:11). Apparently, Abraham and his children have retained their identity as persons, and we will know them. Even in *sheol*—the place of the dead—the rich man had self-recognition and a memory of his spiritually needy brothers (see Luke 16:19–31). However, we must admit that the Sadducees raised a valid point. In heaven, how will people sort out the various relationships—marriages, adoptions, divorces, enemies—that they have had in this life?

We may never figure it out. Maybe relationships are so altered in heaven that the problems we see from our point of view will seem silly from that perspective. Maybe all relationships will be raised to the level of marriage relationships—or maybe higher. Maybe our preoccupation with sex and jealousy gets in the way of our understanding of heaven. Perhaps Jesus needs to tell us, "I have spoken to you of earthly things and you do not believe; how then will you believe if I speak of heavenly things?" (John 3:12). Our answers are incomplete. Most of us cannot imagine heaven without knowing our loved ones, so perhaps our human understanding is normal. We do know this: heaven will be better than we can think or imagine. So perhaps imagining what would be very best for us now is a fair way to imagine heaven. Such speculation may be inaccurate, but it at least heads in the general direction of heaven. Heaven is a place of wonderful bliss.

Communal Life Everlasting

No matter how we imagine heaven, we must say that it is not a private compartment where we go to have our individualistic dreams fulfilled. Maybe it is forgivable that Kenny imagines heaven as fly-fishing by himself on his own personal stream, but this is not how the Bible pictures heaven. Heaven is not a private compartment for each person but a massive gathering of the people of God. Heaven is a *peopled* place. It is a "new Jerusalem," a city coming down from God. In the book of Revelation, there are no solos sung, and nobody worships alone in the mountains with their iPod. We presume that those of us who dearly love the solitude of the mountains will be suitably sanctified before entering heaven so we can love a crowded city just as well! In heaven, worship is corporate; great throngs of people of all tribes and nations and races worship and praise God. The person who despises collective worship will not want to be in heaven. Of course, we should remember that we will be *glorified* before entering heaven. Therefore, if you are a peevish worshipper who often grumbles at the music, you can expect to be changed before entering heaven so you will be able to accept heaven's strange worship style.

180

A city, a banquet, a feast, endless worship—these are all communal pictures of heaven. It should be obvious to us because of who is going there: the church. The church goes to heaven. The entire church—all Christians from everywhere and from all ages.

Peter, John, Mary the mother of Jesus, and Mary Magdalene will be there. My dad and your mother and our brothers and sisters, sons and daughters, and everyone who is a part of God's people will be there. Your deceased spouse and your son who drowned in the lake and your daughter who died in an auto accident will also be there if they are in God's family. John Wesley and John Calvin and the John the Apostle will sit down together. Abraham and Isaac and Jacob and you and me. All who are God's children will be there. It will be one gigantic reunion, one eternal thanksgiving dinner. One everlasting worship service where we will not complain about the music. If we cannot sing a single note, God will enable us to sing "Holy! Holy! Holy!" If our back aches when we stand longer than a half hour, God will give us a new back so we could stand for an eternity—and like it. If we do not like crowds or people unlike us now, God will have finished his work in us by then and we will love the gigantic throngs of God's people of all races and tribes gathered about his throne. Heaven is a communal place.

THE GOAL OF LIFE

The Bible gives us a very different way to think about heaven: heaven is the goal of life. How alien this is to today's view of heaven as a reward. We Christians sometimes get so earthbound that this way of thinking escapes us. Consider how it would change your life if you began thinking of heaven as life's goal rather than as a reward. Think this through for a moment. For what were we created? To live here? To eat pizza, drink lemonade, and watch movies? To get up and go to work and make money, eat ice cream cones, build houses, and write books? Is this the purpose of life just to live on earth and do whatever seems to bring happiness? Not at all. What is the purpose of life? The atheist answers that question with earthbound answers such as "To eat, drink and be merry—and then to die." Christians give another answer: "We are created for worship and fellowship with God and others forever." We will find this destiny most perfectly in heaven, not on earth. Heaven is the goal of life.

Earth is a short waypoint on our route to eternity. We are just passing through. We are pilgrims and strangers, citizens of another world. We live here now, but soon—very soon—we are going to see the King. We shall behold him. We shall see him as he is. When we see Christ face to face, this revelation will completely change us. We shall be like him (see 1 John 3:2–3). In heaven we will be able to do what we have yearned to do all our lives—worship and commune with God and each other perfectly. We long for intimate times with God and others, yet they usually fall short of our longings. Actually, they *always* fall short. Life here, even in the church, is not everything God intends it to be. Church members clash, our daily devotions are disrupted, our mind wanders, and God seems distant. That is now. In the *then* we will commune with God and each other forever, perfectly and

182

completely. There will be no arguments. There will be no strife, bickering, or division, no pain, death, sin, or even temptation. Our relationship with God will be complete and communal and ever-lasting, and maybe we will even make continual progress in our growing love for God and others. We will experience one eternal communion of fellowship and harmony. It will never end. When we've been there ten thousand years, we will have not yet used up any days.

Heaven is the climax of salvation; it is more than a reward for God's faithful. Heaven is what being a Christian is all about. In heaven, we will become what we were meant to be—fully human, fully holy, fully loving, in full union with God and others. We were not just saved from something but were saved for something—for heaven. It is our destiny, desire, and goal in life. We who were lost and without hope, far from God, were brought inside and made new. Now we are headed for eternal fellowship with God the Father, Son, and Holy Spirit in the life everlasting. In heaven, we will know God. This is what heaven is about. If we were not inter-ested in knowing God, heaven would be hell to us. Those who despise the church today would consider heaven punishment. However, those of us who love God and the church will delight in being there. We shall know him. Jesus said, "This is eternal life, that they may know you, the only true God, and Jesus Christ whom you have sent" (John 17:3). This is why we learn to know God bet-ter now: we are getting ready for heaven. Yet we can only begin to know him now. Then we shall behold him fully. This is why heaven is the goal of this life. Knowing God is the goal worth pursuing, and heaven is the only place we can fully accomplish that goal.

WHAT ABOUT US

What shall we say? How shall we live as Christians who believe in the life everlasting? We live differently than the world. We do. We Christians hold material possessions lightly, knowing that possessions all melt away and we are taking none with us. We attend church, go to Sunday school, and start Bible studies so we can learn more about God. That is our primary occupation in life today and will be in heaven. We Christians put up with irritating people in our church because we know we will spend eternity with them. We chuckle that God will finish his work in them before they enter heaven but quickly laugh aloud, knowing God has even more finishing work to do in us. We ask him to do some of that work now, so attending church can be what he intended it to be, a foretaste of God's glory.

184

We Christians live our lives in light of heaven. Life here is but the beginning of everlasting life. Suffering is temporary and earthbound. Anxious news reports of murders and terrorism and wars do not make us tremble. We are just passing through this world. We are headed home. We are citizens of heaven and only living here until our visas run out. Since we know that eternal life is available to all, we use our short time here to be ambassadors for Christ. We recruit others to become citizens of heaven so we can take them with us. We Christians really believe there is an afterlife. We expect to someday be reunited with our bodies and spend eternity in the presence of God and each other. It will be bliss. Heaven is not a reward for living right or even for having faith; it is the goal of life. There we will love God and enjoy him forever, and love and enjoy each other in perfect harmony and love. In heaven, we will all be able to perfectly keep the two greatest commandments: to love God with all our heart, mind, soul, and strength, and to love others completely.

Thus, we come to the endless end of the Creed. The Christian story started with God the Father, Son, and Holy Spirit in perfect love and fellowship. It ends with our being brought into that eternal perfect love and fellowship. There was perfect communion and companionship in the beginning, and there will be perfect communion and companionship in the end—and this time we are included. All our life on earth is but a cover page. Death for us is merely turning that page to chapter 1. Yet this book has no end, for we will live forever with God and each other. We will remember God's works and commune with the Father through bridal union with Christ by the Holy Spirit. We will participate in the union and love of the Holy Trinity.

Out of love, God created the world. Out of love, God sent his Son. Out of love, he provided a way to draw those of us on the

185

outside to come in. Out of love, he invited us into his perfect and divine fellowship and communion. God became humanity so that humanity might share in divinity. We are going to heaven to live with God and each other forever. The Christian story ends up where it began—in eternal and continual unity, love, and fellowship. The goal of living now is the goal of living then: to know God and love him forever. What wondrous love!

PRAYER

I confess I don't think much about heaven.
I need to ponder it more.
Still, I believe it is true.
Everlasting life.
With you.
Forever.
Why did you plan such an ending,
an end that has no end?

I know.
It's because of your love, which is endless.
Endless love brings an endless end.
I anticipate seeing your face,
dwelling in your presence forever.
We'll sing of your love and your grace.
I believe, Lord.
I believe in the life everlasting.
I believe.
Amen.

OTHER BOOKS BY KEITH DRURY

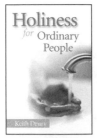

Holiness for Ordinary People
A delightfully written book describing how an ordinary Christian can enter into the experience of being a fully devoted follow of Jesus Christ, based on John Wesley's understanding of sanctification.

With Unveiled Faces: Experience Intimacy with God through Spiritual Disciplines
A practical description of the personal and private disciplines of the Christian life that become the means of grace God uses for remaking us into his image. A popular study book for small groups and classes.

There Is No I in Church:
Moving Beyond Individual Spirituality to Experience God's Power in the Church
This companion book to *With Unveiled Faces* focuses on the corporate spiritual disciplines—those means of grace we experience with other Christians. Also a very popular study book for small groups and Sunday school classes.

The Call of a Lifetime:
Is the Ministry God's Plan for Your Life?
A helpful book describing the work and calling of a minister; especially designed for younger people pondering God's call on their lives.

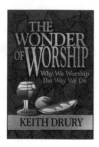

The Wonder of Worship:
Why We Worship the Way We Do
The fascinating story of how the elements of worship we see today developed over time.